T0350512

Electricity Access in Sub-Saharan Africa

Uptake, Reliability, and Complementary Factors for Economic Impact

Moussa P. Blimpo and Malcolm Cosgrove-Davies

A copublication of the Agence française de développement and the World Bank

ISBN (paper): 978-1-4648-1361-0
ISBN (electronic): 978-1-4648-1377-1
DOI: 10.1596/978-1-4648-1361-0

Cover photo: Photographer is my life. / Getty Images. Used with the permission of Photographer is my life. / Getty Images. Further permission required for reuse.

Cover design: Bill Pragluski, Critical Stages.

Library of Congress Cataloging-in-Publication Data has been requested.

Africa Development Forum Series

The **Africa Development Forum Series** was created in 2009 to focus on issues of significant relevance to Sub-Saharan Africa's social and economic development. Its aim is both to record the state of the art on a specific topic and to contribute to ongoing local, regional, and global policy debates. It is designed specifically to provide practitioners, scholars, and students with the most up-to-date research results while highlighting the promise, challenges, and opportunities that exist on the continent.

The series is sponsored by Agence française de développement and the World Bank. The manuscripts chosen for publication represent the highest quality in each institution and have been selected for their relevance to the development agenda. Working together with a shared sense of mission and interdisciplinary purpose, the two institutions are committed to a common search for new insights and new ways of analyzing the development realities of the Sub-Saharan Africa region.

Advisory Committee Members

Agence française de développement
Gaël Giraud, Chief Economist
Thomas Melonio, Executive Director, Innovations, Research and Knowledge Directorate
Pierre Icard, Director, Head of Knowledge Department on Sustainable Development
Sophie Chauvin, Head, Edition and Publication Division
Hélène Djoufelkit, Deputy Head, Research Department

World Bank
Albert G. Zeufack, Chief Economist, Africa Region
Markus P. Goldstein, Lead Economist, Africa Region

Sub-Saharan Africa

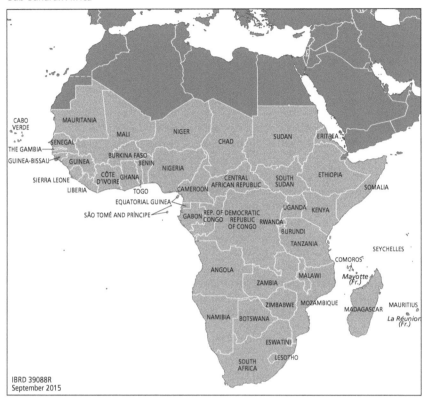

CABO VERDE
MAURITANIA
MALI
NIGER
CHAD
SUDAN
ERITREA
THE GAMBIA
SENEGAL
GUINEA-BISSAU
GUINEA
BURKINA FASO
BENIN
NIGERIA
CENTRAL AFRICAN REPUBLIC
SOUTH SUDAN
ETHIOPIA
SIERRA LEONE
CÔTE D'IVOIRE
GHANA
TOGO
CAMEROON
SOMALIA
LIBERIA
EQUATORIAL GUINEA
SÃO TOMÉ AND PRÍNCIPE
GABON
REP. OF CONGO
DEMOCRATIC REPUBLIC OF CONGO
UGANDA
KENYA
RWANDA
BURUNDI
TANZANIA
SEYCHELLES
COMOROS
ANGOLA
ZAMBIA
MALAWI
Mayotte (Fr.)
ZIMBABWE
MOZAMBIQUE
MADAGASCAR
MAURITIUS
La Réunion (Fr.)
NAMIBIA
BOTSWANA
ESWATINI
LESOTHO
SOUTH AFRICA

IBRD 39088R
September 2015

Titles in the Africa Development Forum Series

Tourism in Africa: Harnessing Tourism for Growth and Improved Livelihoods (2014) by Iain Christie, Eneida Fernandes, Hannah Messerli, and Louise Twining-Ward

* *Safety Nets in Africa: Effective Mechanisms to Reach the Poor and Most Vulnerable* «Les fi lets sociaux en Afrique: Méthodes effi caces pour cibler les populations pauvres et vulnérables en Afrique» (2015) edited by Carlo del Ninno and Bradford Mills

* *Land Delivery Systems in West African Cities: The Example of Bamako, Mali* «Le système d'approvisionnement en terres dans les villes d'Afrique de l'Ouest: L'exemple de Bamako» (2015) by Alain Durand-Lasserve, Maÿlis Durand-Lasserve, and Harris Selod

Enhancing the Climate Resilience of Africa's Infrastructure: The Power and Water Sectors (2015) edited by Raffaello Cervigni, Rikard Liden, James E. Neumann, and Kenneth M. Strzepek

* *Africa's Demographic Transition: Dividend or Disaster?* «La transition demograpique de lAfrique» (2015) edited by David Canning, Sangeeta Raja, and Abdo S. Yazbeck

The Challenge of Fragility and Security in West Africa (2015) by Alexandre Marc, Neelam Verjee, and Stephen Mogaka

Highways to Success or Byways to Waste: Estimating the Economic Benefits of Roads in Africa (2015) by Ali A. Rubaba, Federico Barra, Claudia Berg, Richard Damania, John Nash, and Jason Russ

Confronting Drought in Africa's Drylands: Opportunities for Enhancing Resilience (2016) edited by Raffaello Cervigni and Michael Morris

Reaping Richer Returns: Public Spending Priorities for African Agriculture Productivity Growth (2017) by Aparajita Goyal and John Nash

Mining in Africa: Are Local Communities Better Off? (2017) by Punam Chuhan-Pole, Andrew L. Dabalen, and Bryan Christopher Land

Realizing the Full Potential of Social Safety Nets in Africa (2018) edited by Kathleen Beegle, Aline Coudouel, and Emma Monsalve

Facing Forward: Schooling for Learning in Africa (2018) by Sajitha Bashir, Marlaine Lockheed, Elizabeth Ninan, and Jee-Peng Tan

* Available in French

All books in the Africa Development Forum Series are available for free at https://openknowledge.worldbank.org/handle/10986/2150

Contents

Maps

Tables

Foreword

Access to reliable electricity is the backbone of any modern economy. It is even more important with the digital revolution. If African nations want to see their economies transform, the issue of electricity must be tackled head-on. Access is only the starting point, however. Expansion needs investment, too, and for that, utilities must make money. Yet all over the region, utilities are running at a loss.

This report takes a broader look at the issue to show that the problem in Africa is not power but poverty. It shows that reliability, affordability, and coordination are the links missing between making utilities viable and expanding their consumer base. Reliability and affordability go hand in glove: blackouts and brownouts are common in Africa. Reliable electricity would persuade consumers that electricity is a service worth paying for, and more consumers would bring down the cost of producing electricity.

This is precisely where this report offers ideas on the way forward. By carefully examining the obstacles to increasing popular demand for electrical power, it highlights the constraints to consumer expansion on the continent. These constraints include irregular household income, high (and repeated) connection charges, tedious application processes, and a quality of housing that does not always meet the requirements needed for connections to the main grid.

Prepaid meters can help; so can flexible payment plans, ready boards, and smart metering. But these are simply ways of adapting to systemic problems. What is needed now is to tackle the problems themselves. The report argues that access to electricity cannot be a stand-alone goal; what is needed is to place the *productive* use of electrification center stage. This means countries need to invest in other aspects of their infrastructure at the same time as they invest in electricity, such as in improving access to markets through better roads and expanding credit for new businesses. In this way, electricity could energize agriculture in rural areas and industry in urban areas.

The World Bank is taking steps to increase this type of cross-sectoral coordination and focusing on large projects with meaningful impacts. Technological progress may soon allow off-grid systems to provide enough electricity for productive use at much lower cost, giving African countries the opportunity to leapfrog the slow stages of electrification with which other continents have had to contend.

To make a start, policies need to evolve to the point where investing in infrastructure in Africa attracts more private investment and more public-private partnerships. The World Bank stands ready to assist countries embarking on the reforms to make both of these possible. This report shows that, above all, to generate income, create jobs, and alleviate poverty in Africa, electricity has to be part of a package. On its own, it may not be enough to make a difference.

Hafez Ghanem
Vice President for Africa
World Bank
Washington, DC

Makhtar Diop
Vice President for Infrastructure
World Bank
Washington, DC

Acknowledgments

This regional study was prepared by a team led by Moussa P. Blimpo (Senior Economist, Office of the Chief Economist, Africa Region, World Bank) and Malcolm Cosgrove-Davies (Global Lead, Energy and Extractives Global Practice, World Bank) and under the overall guidance of Albert G. Zeufack, Chief Economist for the Africa Region of the World Bank. The contributors to the background research included Justice Tei Mensah (Swedish University of Agricultural Sciences), Agnieszka Postepska (University of Groningen), Shaun McCrae (Instituto Tecnológico Autónomo de México), Jevgenijs Steinbuks (Development Research Group, Environment and Energy, World Bank), Samba Mbaye (Université Gaston Berger, Senegal), Michael Minges (Consultant, World Bank), Kenneth Opalo (Georgetown University), and Musiliu Oseni (Regulator, Republic of Nigeria). The team included Kabir Malik (Energy and Extractives Global Practice, World Bank), Aly Sanoh (Poverty Global Practice, World Bank), Subodh Mathur (Energy and Extractives Global Practice, World Bank), Wilfried A. Kouamé (Office of the Chief Economist, Africa Region, World Bank), Ruifan Shi (World Bank), and Yanbin Xu (Office of the Chief Economist, Africa Region, World Bank). The team would like to thank Dana Rysankova, Elisa Portale, and the Multi-Tier Framework (MTF) team of the World Bank for fruitful collaboration throughout the study and the MTF data collection processes.

The team benefited from the advice and contributions of extended team members, including Taryn Dinkelman (Dartmouth College), Kenneth Houangbedji (Agence française de développement), Kelsey Jack (Tufts University), and Elvira Morella (Senior Energy Specialist, Energy and Extractives Global Practice, World Bank).

The team benefited from the guidance of the Advisory Board composed of Sudeshna G. Banerjee (Practice Manager, Energy and Extractives Global Practice, World Bank), Andrew L. Dabalen (Practice Manager, Poverty Global Practice, World Bank), Vivien Foster (Global Lead, Energy and Extractives Global Practice, World Bank), Lucio Monari (Director, Energy and Extractives

Global Practice, World Bank), Michael Toman (Research Manager, Development Research Group, Environment and Energy, World Bank), and Catherine Wolfram (Cora Jane Flood Professor of Business Administration, Haas School of Business, University of California at Berkeley). The team thanks the Advisory Board for their support of the research report.

The team is grateful to the peer reviewers for their insightful comments, which helped improve the overall quality of the study. The reviewers were Marianne Fay (Chief Economist, Sustainable Practice Group, World Bank), Jörg Peters (Leibniz Institute for Economic Research), Michael Toman (Research Manager, Development Research Group, Environment and Energy, World Bank), Fan Zhang (Senior Economist, Office of the Chief Economist, South Asia, World Bank), and other anonymous reviewers.

About the Authors

Moussa P. Blimpo is a Senior Economist in the Office of the Chief Economist for the Africa Region (AFRCE) of the World Bank. Prior to this, he was an assistant professor of economics and international studies at the University of Oklahoma. His research interests cover a range of policy-relevant questions concerning African economies. His recent research and publications address issues of electricity access in Sub-Saharan Africa, the role of disruptive technologies on the prospects of African economies to leapfrog and address key development challenges, and human capital acquisition in African countries. He holds a PhD in economics from New York University and spent two years as a postdoctoral fellow at Stanford University's Institute for Economic Policy Research (SIEPR). He founded, and led between 2011 and 2015, the Center for Research and Opinion Polls (CROP), a think tank based in Togo.

Malcolm Cosgrove-Davies (Mac) started with the World Bank in 1992 as a contract employee for the Asia Alternative Energy Unit (ASTAE), focusing on rural and renewable energy in South and East Asia. He formally joined the World Bank in 1999 as a Senior Energy Specialist. He worked in the Africa region for nearly 10 years; he then returned to South Asia for three years before serving as Energy Practice Manager in Latin America and the Caribbean for three years and subsequently as the Global Lead for Energy Access.

His career involved extensive experience across the energy sector, including team leadership and supporting roles covering grid and off-grid energy access, small and large renewable energy, energy sector reform and restructuring, emergency power, hydropower, thermal power, and transmission. His passion for the energy access agenda was nurtured throughout his career, including highlights such as the Sri Lanka Energy Services Delivery Project, the Lao Rural Electrification Project, and the Uganda Energy for Rural Transformation Program. He sought to lead the World Bank's Energy Practice in expanding and further leveraging its energy access work, including building effective links within and outside the institution. He retired in April 2018.

Abbreviations

CFAF	CFA franc
CI	confidence interval
DHS	Demographic and Health Surveys
EAPP	Eastern Africa Power Pool
EVN	Vietnam Electricity, state utility of Vietnam
GDP	gross domestic product
GPT	general-purpose technology
GWh	gigawatt hours
HDI	Human Development Index
HH	households
IBRD	International Bank for Reconstruction and Development
ICT	information and communication technology
IDA	International Development Association
IEA	International Energy Agency
IRD	Integrated Rural Development
kW	kilowatt
kWh	kilowatt hour
lmhr	lumen-hour
LSMS	Living Standards Measurement Study
MSEs	micro and small enterprises
MSMEs	micro, small, and medium-size enterprises
MTF	Multi-Tier Framework
MWh	megawatt hour
PC	personal computer
PPP	purchasing power parity

PRODUSE	productive use of electricity
RF	Rwanda franc
RISE	Regulatory Indicators for Sustainable Energy
SDGs	Sustainable Development Goals
SHEP	Self-Help Electrification Program
SSA	Sub-Saharan Africa
TFP	total factor productivity
TWh	terawatt hour
US$	U.S. dollars
W	watt
WDI	World Development Indicators
Wh	watt hour
WTP	willingness to pay

Overview

The rate of access to electricity in Sub-Saharan Africa (hereafter Africa or SSA) is substantially lower than what it could be, considering levels of income and the electric grid footprint. This lack of access to electricity imposes significant constraints on modern economic activities, provision of public services, and quality of life, as well as on adoption of new technologies in various sectors such as education, agriculture, and finance. Not only is the 43 percent access rate much lower than that in comparable regions (as well as the global access rate of 87 percent), but the total number of people without electricity has increased in recent decades as population growth has outpaced growth in electrification. Furthermore, the access rate is much lower in rural Africa (25 percent).

Uptake and Demand, Often Neglected, Are Key to Addressing Access Deficits

Contrary to common perception, demand-side challenges are as much or more of an obstacle to greater electrification than supply-side constraints. The share of households that live near the electric grid but that are not connected is high, with a median uptake of only 57 percent for 20 countries for which comparable Living Standards Measurement Study (LSMS) data are available. This low uptake is a critical reason for the access deficit. Uptake rates vary across countries; they are high in a few countries such as Cameroon, Gabon, Nigeria, and South Africa, and very low in other countries including Liberia, Malawi, Niger, Sierra Leone, and Uganda. Uptake rates vary within countries, too, with a high concentration in urban and peri-urban areas. For example, only the central region of Uganda, which includes the capital, Kampala, has an uptake rate exceeding 50 percent (Blimpo, Postepska, and Xu 2018). A study conducted in 150 communities in western Kenya finds that electrification uptake remained very low, including for relatively well-off households, averaging 6 percent for households and 22 percent for businesses (Lee et al. 2016). Similarly, an evaluation of a large electrification project in Tanzania finds that the number of new connections was less than one-third of what was initially projected (Chaplin et al. 2017).

Demand and supply constraints to electricity access are interlinked. However, a significant share of the access gap can be explained by demand factors that vary in importance across countries. An analysis of 31 countries in Africa (Blimpo, Postepska, and Xu 2018) reveals that pure demand-related factors account for about two-fifths of the access gap, with significant variations across countries and subregions. Demand considerations account for 56 percent of the overall constraint in lower-middle-income countries, compared with 30 percent in low-income countries, where infrastructure development lags further behind.

To make electricity expansion financially viable and to encourage investment, uptake and utilization need to be higher. For example, if all households living within range of the electrical grid were connected to the grid, access rates would be well over 60 percent, on average, in Africa and nearly double the current rate in many countries. Why are these households not connected, and what kind of incentives would get them connected? This situation underscores the need for a deeper understanding of demand-side constraints to uptake.

Low uptake is affected by the maximum amount people are willing to pay. For example, when households in Rwanda were offered three price and payment options, 88 percent did not accept any of the options. When disaggregating the results by social and economic status using a wide range of variables, uptake was low nearly across the board. Similarly, willingness to pay in Liberia fell from 90 percent to 60 percent when the connection charges moved from zero to US$10; it fell to about 10 percent when the proposed connection charges exceeded US$50.

While Removing Key Demand Barriers Can Bring Some Gains in Access, Most Are Often Symptoms, Not Root Causes of Low Access

Uptake is not always feasible for consumers because they face multiple constraints. Framing the demand for electricity in Africa from the standpoint of basic consumer theory helps organize potential constraints to uptake under three related categories: (1) price, (2) household income, and (3) the expected benefit from electricity uptake.

- *Connection charges and the process of getting connected are critical entry point barriers and suggest an important policy lever for higher uptake, but they are often not fully understood.* Connection charges are, on average, high relative to the level of income in most countries. Additionally, based on evidence from 10 countries in Africa focusing on recently connected households, other factors play a role: (1) the connection requirement and process are often standard and not designed to alleviate the constraints that the poor face; (2) the process entails long waiting times, often exceeding 10 weeks; and (3) although the cost of connection is often thought of as fixed, there are significant variations across households within the same country when wiring and transaction costs are considered. The variation tends to be regressive, thus exacerbating affordability for the poor (Blimpo et al. 2018).

- *Although the level of income matters for uptake, income flow and predictability are tied to households' willingness to connect to electricity services.* A recurring payment of even a small amount can constitute a major problem for households that generate their income on an irregular basis. Prepaid meters can play a crucial role in circumventing this constraint. Flexible mechanisms for bill payment, mirroring income fluctuations, could further address this issue.

- *Electricity connection via conventional AC (alternating current) supply requires minimum building standards that many existing houses do not meet.* There are technologies, such as ready boards, that make it possible to connect even substandard houses. Coordination between regulators in the housing and electricity sectors can help ensure that the requirements for building permits conform to the standards required for electrical connection.

Without Addressing Structural Challenges, Utilities Will Continue to Face Financial Disincentives to Streamline and Remove Access Barriers

Increasing uptake more rapidly will require that challenges caused by below-cost tariffs be resolved. In most countries in Africa, connecting an additional household is unprofitable, diminishing utilities' incentives to streamline the connection process and remove access barriers. Distribution utilities in most African countries would incur losses from adding one more consumer at the lifeline tariff (without considering connection costs or other charges). Evidence suggests that without raising tariffs, distribution utilities in many countries cannot break even with connection fees lower than US$200. Under these conditions, high connection charges and low access result from regulated electricity tariffs that are not high enough and from low consumption.

Even when access is achieved, consumption levels in Africa are low, meaning that users are getting only limited benefits and utilities cannot recover their costs. Per capita residential consumption of electricity averaged 483 kilowatt hours in 2014, which is roughly the amount of electricity needed to power a 50-watt lightbulb continuously for a year. Both the access rate and consumption level are lower than they should be when countries in Africa are benchmarked against countries from other regions with similar levels of income per capita.

Sustained Development Gains Can Only Be Achieved by Focusing on Enhancing Economic Impact through Firms and Productive Uses

Sustained progress in electricity access will need to go hand in hand with job creation and income generation. Productive uses of electricity enhance firms' and households' ability to pay. High capacity and reliable electricity are needed for productive uses that generate economic impact and financial benefits for the utility. Technological progress may soon allow off-grid electricity systems, particularly those that can be powered by efficient motors, to provide enough electrical capacity for productive uses at a significantly lower cost. Off-grid systems would provide an opportunity for many African countries to leapfrog economic development, particularly in rural areas. Even though alleviation of demand constraints will increase uptake, a large share of the population still cannot afford to connect or use a reasonable amount of electricity, let alone purchase appliances that can help generate income. Accordingly, it is essential to think beyond uptake and promote productive use through the provision of reliable electricity with adequate capacity. Electrification plays a crucial role in creating opportunities for income-generating activities. Without electricity contributing to job creation and rising incomes, the overwhelming majority of the population cannot afford meaningful usage with their current level of income. Aligning electrification rollout to job creation is also a crucial way to attract more investment and improve the financial viability of the sector.

Prioritizing Reliability Would Boost Uptake and Enhance Economic Impact

Households and firms endure several hours a day without access to power. Even in instances in which power is available, brownouts are prevalent, thereby limiting end users' potential utilization of electricity. In Liberia, more than half of connected households report that they never have electricity. Sierra Leone and Uganda also have severe reliability challenges, with more than 30 percent reporting never having electricity despite being connected to the grid. In some countries—including Burundi, Ghana, Guinea, Liberia, Nigeria, and Zimbabwe—more than half of connected households reported receiving electricity less than 50 percent of the time in 2014.

The cost of electricity in Africa is the highest in the world, yet regulated tariffs are often below cost-recovery levels, contributing to reliability challenges. The maintenance and investment needed to provide reliable services are constrained. In 25 of the 29 countries in Africa with recent data, less than one-third of firms have reliable access to electricity. More than two-thirds of firms in these countries experience electricity outages, with direct implications for their operations.

Reliable electricity can contribute to increasing uptake. Reliability of electricity is positively associated with uptake across and within countries. Countries with high uptake of electricity also tend to have a higher level of reliability and vice versa. Investment to address reliability should be given higher priority because poor quality poses a significant constraint on economic impact as well. The quality of services may be worse than what is perceived, and differences in the level of quality mirror income inequality. Without adequate quality, the economic impact of electricity will be significantly constrained even when all complementary factors are in place. Low economic impact caused by inadequate quality will also contribute to keeping demand and uptake low. This effect is also true for off-grid electricity solutions, where capacity, durability, and reliability are crucial to household uptake.

Impact is affected by reliability. Analysis of firm data indicates that for every percentage point increase in the frequency of electricity outages experienced by firms, output declines by 3.3 percent. Similarly, the effect on firms' revenue is nontrivial: a percentage point increase in outage frequency results in a 2.7 percent loss in firm revenue.

Countries in Africa could increase tax revenues by more than 4 percent per year solely by resolving issues related to the reliability of electricity. The provision of quality infrastructure services, such as reliable electricity, is a mechanism through which governments in developing countries can enhance tax revenues. Evidence suggests that connection to the grid can potentially signal government's commitment to the provision of social infrastructure and services and thereby reinforce the sense of an implicit fiscal pact between citizens and their governments. The impact of the reliability of electricity on taxation occurs through two channels: the effect on citizens' incentive to pay taxes, and tax revenue losses caused by the negative impact of outages on the productive sectors of the economy.

Provision of Complementary Factors Is Needed to Maximize the Economic Impact of Reliable Electricity

Electrification policies should transition from a stand-alone power sector concern to a more coordinated approach whereby the provision of electrification is complemented with other necessary infrastructure and access to public services. The provision of electricity should be accompanied by elements such as market access and financial services, which will ensure that the various segments of the local economy function effectively to stimulate economic development. A more coordinated approach should be adopted in which increased electrification is complemented by the infrastructure and access to public services necessary to enhance the economic impact. Investment should not target electrification alone; it should be coordinated with investments in the provision of complementary factors.

New data on Rwanda find that skills and access to markets have a positive effect on the impact of electricity for job creation in the nonfarm sector. Access to credit and public services spurs the impact of electricity in boosting household incomes from farm and nonfarm sources. Skills training programs and the removal of barriers to market access will increase entrepreneurial activities so that electricity services can be better exploited for productive use. The identification of the drivers of economic impact should motivate future research to help inform policies and strengthen the rationale for the rollout of electrification as well as the sequencing of investments for electrification and its complementary factors.

Electrification must also be equitable between urban and rural areas. Many rural areas have significant untapped economic potential—off-season farming and value-added agro-processing—that could be unleashed through the provision of electricity. This discrepancy is all the more relevant given that, in many African countries, the majority of the population resides in rural areas and the agriculture sector employs the majority of the labor force.

Key Overarching Policy Implications

Electrification is a long-term investment that lays the foundation for development. Countries that have the financial capacity should plan and roll out electrification without delay. Electrification in Africa needs to focus on enhancing the economic capabilities of communities as the best way to achieve faster and sustainable development progress while addressing broad challenges (including affordability, low consumption, and financial viability of utilities) and ensuring equitable provision between urban and rural areas.

Rapid progress in electrification requires that governments rethink their strategies for the sector based on the key fundamental principles discussed as well as being conscious of key trends that may affect electrification rollout.

Experiences elsewhere suggest that the centerpiece of successful electrification rollout is preparation and implementation of a national electrification strategy addressing in a systematic and coordinated manner the institutional, technical, and financial aspects involved in electrification. A recent study (World Bank 2017) finds that only half of 35 countries in Africa have officially approved electrification plans. An adequate regulatory framework will also help attract investment to fill the gap where public funding falls short. Many of the poorest performers in an index measuring electricity regulation are in Africa, suggesting that institutional reform and human and financial capacity assistance are needed. Additionally, Africa is faced with key megatrends that need to be factored into electrification efforts, specifically *urbanization, technological change,* and *regional integration, as well as climate change.* Significant uncertainty surrounds the evolution and timing of these factors, which complicates electrification planning. All power sector planning and development should take into account the extent and impact of these trends.

Several essential policy considerations must be addressed for boosting access, increasing uptake, improving reliability, and raising impacts (see figure O.1).

- *Recognize that electrification is a long-term investment and a necessary input for economic transformation.* Plans to increase access should not be evaluated based only on short-term benefits. African countries have underinvested in electricity, even though in many countries, rents from natural resources could be an essential source for financing electrification. The short-term benefits of electrification are unlikely to cover its costs; in the long run, however, electrification is a key driver of economic transformation. Delaying electrification has a high opportunity cost because the lack of electricity impedes modern technology adoption and lowers the quality of delivery of services such as health care, education, and other public services. It may also negatively affect how urbanization unfolds. Hence, it is important to find ways to finance the upfront costs of electrification that may not yield short-term results. In this regard, electrification may be viewed as a time-consistent way to save or invest natural resource proceeds for future generations.

- *Address demand constraints at all stages of the electrification process.* Addressing demand constraints is essential to raising uptake. Households in Africa often cannot afford connection fees and consumption tariffs because of lack of adequate and regular income. Households face other demand constraints such as inadequate housing quality and costs associated with internal wiring—in addition to the inability to afford appliances that need electricity. Some of these constraints can be addressed by the deployment of technologies such as smart meters, prepayment solutions, and ready boards to circumvent housing quality requirements. Better application of lifeline tariffs can also help: some middle- and high-income households are on reduced tariffs even though they could afford to pay more, while those sharing a connection are not benefiting from lifeline tariffs. Also, well-off households and firms might be willing to pay more if reliability were improved. However, it is important to recognize that these constraints are often symptoms rather than root causes of low uptake. Addressing the root causes will require focusing on enhancing economic impacts, with the following considerations:

Figure O.1 A Framework for Addressing the Electricity Access Deficit in Africa

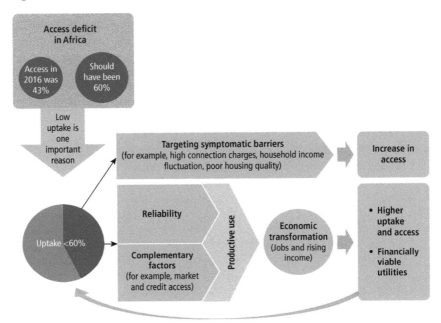

- *Target and promote productive use* so that electrification will raise household income, enhance household ability to pay, help the financial viability of utilities through higher consumption, and feed back into public finances through taxes for reinvestment. This goal will, however, require reliability and the provision of complementary factors.

- *Prioritize reliability*, whenever access is provided, because reliability will be crucial if electricity provision is going to pay for itself. Access rates alone should not be the sole measure of progress because universal access may not deliver its full promise if *quality* and *reliability* continue to be poor, with a significant strain on economies in Africa and the livelihood of their people.

- *Coordinate with other sectors to take advantage of complementarities* and the provision of appropriate inputs to productive economic activities. For example, coordinating with development initiatives (road infrastructure investment, access to finance, skills development, public service delivery, for instance) could help prioritize where to provide electricity and thereby amplify its economic impact. Technology, such as geographic information system mapping techniques, can be leveraged to improve geospatial planning for electrification rollout.

- *Take advantage of recent technological advances in off-grid solutions to strategically promote productive uses, especially in rural areas.* This objective can be achieved through the adoption of cost-effective solar solutions that can provide sufficient capacity and reliability to support income-generating activities such as off-season farming, value-added agro-processing, and promoting other small businesses (for example, hairdressers, eating establishments, tailors, and others).

References

Blimpo, M. P., K. Gbenyo, C. Meniago, and J. T. Mensah. 2018. "Stylized Facts on the Cost of Household Connection to the Electricity Grid in African Countries." Working Paper, World Bank, Washington, DC.

Blimpo, M. P., A. Postepska, and Y. Xu. 2018. "Why Is Household Electricity Uptake Low in Sub-Saharan Africa?" Working Paper, World Bank, Washington, DC.

Chaplin, D., A. Mamun, A. Protik, J. Schurrer, D. Vohra, K. Bos, H. Burak, L. Meyer, A. Dumitrescu, C. Ksoll, and T. Cook. 2017. "Grid Electricity Expansion in Tanzania by MCC: Findings from a Rigorous Impact Evaluation." Millennium Challenge Corporation, Princeton, NJ.

Lee, K., E. Brewer, C. Christiano, F. Meyo, E. Miguel, M. Podolsky, H. Rosa, and C. Wolfram. 2016. "Barriers to Electrification for 'Under Grid' Households in Rural Kenya." *Development Engineering* 1 (Supplement C): 26–35.

World Bank. 2017. "Regulatory Indicators for Sustainable Energy: A Global Scorecard to Policy Makers." World Bank, Washington, DC.

Chapter 1

Electricity Access in Sub-Saharan Africa: Taking Stock and Looking Forward

It is hard to imagine a growing modern economy or healthy and productive households with a massive shortage of electricity. Yet just over two-fifths of the population in Sub-Saharan Africa (Africa or SSA hereafter) has access to electricity, the lowest of all world regions. The electricity access rate in Africa is substantially lower than it could be, considering the level of income and the electric grid footprint. The lack of access to electricity imposes major constraints on modern economic activities, the provision of public services, the adoption of new technologies, and the quality of life.

Poor State of Electrification Compared with the Rest of the World

There have been concerted efforts and commitments, internationally and within the Africa region, to close the electrification gap by 2030. A recent report reflects this commitment by showing that the progress made between 2010 and 2012 was larger than in the previous decade (World Bank and IEA 2015). However, more accelerated growth is needed to meet the timetable of global targets.

The globally agreed-upon Sustainable Development Goals consider energy to be a vital, cross-cutting element of infrastructure that is critical for achieving many of the Sustainable Development Goals and reducing poverty. The following target is called for in Sustainable Development Goal 7: "By 2030, ensure access to affordable, reliable, sustainable and modern energy for all."[1] However, recent rates of growth in electricity access indicate that Africa will not meet this target.

Although it is imperative to raise the level of access, that alone will be insufficient for electricity to have the needed impact on reducing poverty and raising output. Higher levels of access need to be accompanied by greater consumption and better quality, as well as by affordable prices for consumers and sustainable tariffs for utilities, to achieve economic transformation in the region.

A Large Access Deficit

Although access has been slowly rising, only 42.8 percent of the population in Africa had access to electricity in 2016, far less than any other developing region (figure 1.1, panel a). More than 600 million people in Africa live without electricity, including more than 80 percent of those residing in rural areas. Only two countries in the region, Mauritius and Seychelles, have near universal electricity coverage. Household electricity access is 75 percent or higher in only six nations in Africa. Almost two-thirds of the countries in the region have household access rates of less than 50 percent (figure 1.1, panel b).

Lack of access to electricity is endemic in Africa regardless of income. The region is unique in the world in having the most countries whose level of electrification is below what their income level would predict (figure 1.2). Africa stands out for outliers, such as Botswana, Equatorial Guinea, and Namibia, which should have significantly higher levels of electricity access given their per capita incomes. Overall, the region's average level of electricity access in 2016 could have been 60 percent, given its per capita income, instead of 43 percent.

Given that Africa is well below where it should be in electrification, how fast could the rate of electrification grow? Castellano, Kendall, and Nikomarov (2015) find that access to electricity grows slowly if current levels are less than 20 percent or greater than 80 percent. On average, it takes about 25 years to get from 20 to 80 percent electrification of households, or about 2.4 percentage points per year (figure 1.3, panel a). Some countries are speedier than others: Vietnam took only 9 years, whereas Brazil took more than 40. In Africa, electricity access is growing at well less than the average rate. Access to electricity rose 20 percent during the 25-year period between 1991 and 2016, or just 0.8 percentage point per year. At that rate, the region will not achieve the Sustainable Development Goal target for universal access to electricity by 2030.

Ghana provides an example of an African nation demonstrating that above-average growth is possible (figure 1.3, panel b). In the five-year period 1993–98, access to electricity in households grew by 2.4 percentage points per year, to 43 percent from 31 percent. Growth slowed to just 1.1 percentage points per year between 1998 and 2003. Since then, access grew at 2.4 percentage points per year during 2003–08 and 3.0 percentage points per year during 2008–14. Overall, it took Ghana 21 years to raise household electrification to 78 percent from 31 percent, with an average annual gain of 2.3 percentage points.

Although low access is often used as a proxy for the energy deficit in SSA, the challenges go far beyond the access shortfall. The current state of the electricity sector in most African countries is also characterized by limited consumption, pervasive reliability challenges, prohibitive prices, and utilities in financial distress. These constraints pose a challenge to the region's economic and human development.

Figure 1.1 Access to Electricity

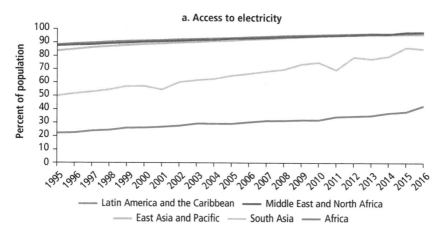

a. Access to electricity

Latin America and the Caribbean —— Middle East and North Africa
—— East Asia and Pacific —— South Asia —— Africa

b. Households with electricity, latest available data (percent)

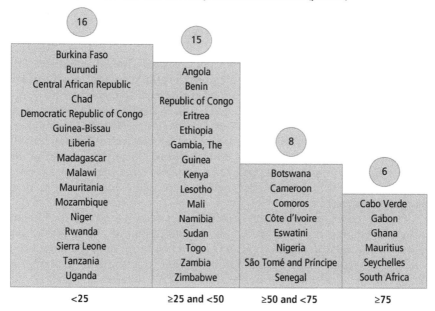

16	15	8	6
Burkina Faso	Angola		
Burundi	Benin		
Central African Republic	Republic of Congo		
Chad	Eritrea		
Democratic Republic of Congo	Ethiopia		
Guinea-Bissau	Gambia, The		
Liberia	Guinea	Botswana	
Madagascar	Kenya	Cameroon	
Malawi	Lesotho	Comoros	Cabo Verde
Mauritania	Mali	Côte d'Ivoire	Gabon
Mozambique	Namibia	Eswatini	Ghana
Niger	Sudan	Nigeria	Mauritius
Rwanda	Togo	São Tomé and Príncipe	Seychelles
Sierra Leone	Zambia	Senegal	South Africa
Tanzania	Zimbabwe		
Uganda			
<25	**≥25 and <50**	**≥50 and <75**	**≥75**

Sources: World Bank World Development Indicators; Demographic and Health Surveys; Multiple Indicator Cluster Surveys; national surveys.
Note: In panel a, high-income countries are excluded. In panel b, recent data are not available for Equatorial Guinea, Somalia, and South Sudan. Latin America and Caribbean and Middle East and North Africa have a near perfect overlap on the figure.

Figure 1.2 **Relation between GDP per Capita and Access to Electricity, 2016**

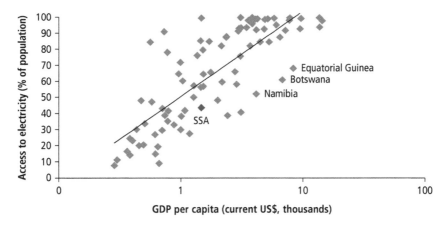

Source: World Bank World Development Indicators 2016.
Note: Figure excludes economies that have already reached 100 percent access. GDP = gross domestic product;
SSA = Sub-Saharan Africa.

Access without Meaningful Consumption Levels Poses Another Challenge

Gross domestic product (GDP) per capita is clearly linked to energy consumption: the higher the income, the greater is the electricity consumption (figure 1.4). Economists have not achieved consensus on whether the direction of the causality is from economic growth to electricity or the other way around (Lemma et al. 2016). Whatever the direction, electricity consumption levels have implications for economic development, as well as for power utilities that require sufficient usage to be sustainable. A study of utilities in the region finds that only two of them have fully recovered their costs (Kojima and Trimble 2016). If access is the enabler of economic transformation, then usage is the driver.

Electric power consumption in Africa is extremely low compared with other developing regions (figure 1.5). The 483 kilowatt hours (kWh) per person consumed in Africa in 2014 is not much more than the amount of electricity needed to power a 50-watt lightbulb continuously for a year (IEA 2014). If African countries were to connect all households quickly, the average level of consumption would remain low because most cannot afford electrical appliances such as air conditioners, refrigerators, and water heaters. Given the prevalence of subsidies, the financial situation of the region's utilities will worsen, threatening their sustainability. It is therefore imperative that as the region makes progress toward universal electricity access, utilization also rises.

Figure 1.3 Number of Years to Increase Access to Electricity to 80 Percent from 20 Percent in Selected Countries, and to 80 Percent from 30 Percent in Ghana

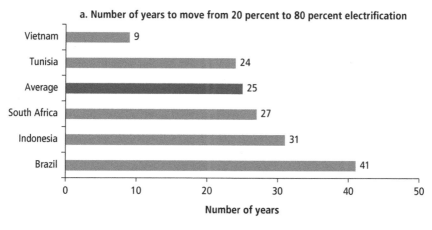

a. Number of years to move from 20 percent to 80 percent electrification

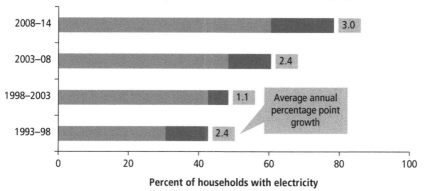

b. Ghana, growth in households with electricity (%)

Sources: Adapted from Castellano, Kendall, and Nikomarov (2015) and Demographic and Health Surveys.

The Cost of Supply Is High, and Most Cannot Afford Cost-Reflective Tariffs

Currently, the unit cost of electricity to consumers in many countries in Africa is more than double the cost in high-income nations such as the United States (US$0.12/kWh) and far higher than in many emerging markets such as India (US$0.08/kWh).[2] In some countries, such as Liberia, the cost of electricity per kilowatt hour is four times that in the United States. In many African countries, it would cost more than 10 percent of per capita GDP to power a refrigerator for a year, a far larger share of most households' income, considering income inequality (figure 1.6). This demonstrates that despite public subsidies, tariffs in

Figure 1.4 Relation between GDP per Capita and Electricity Consumption

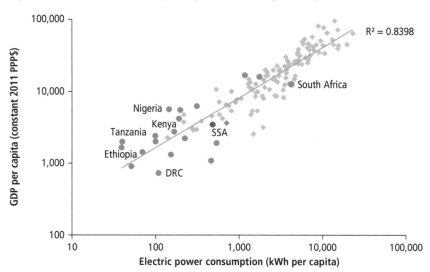

Source: Adapted from World Bank World Development Indicators.
Note: Log scales. Circles represent African countries. GDP = gross domestic product; kWh = kilowatt hours; PPP = purchasing power parity.

Figure 1.5 Electric Power Consumption, 2014

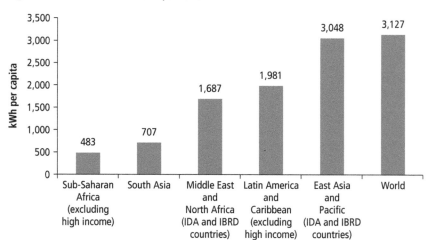

Source: World Bank World Development Indicators 2014.
Note: IBRD = International Bank for Reconstruction and Development; IDA = International Development Association; kWh = kilowatt hours.

Figure 1.6 Price of Powering a Refrigerator for a Year as a Percentage of GDP per Capita

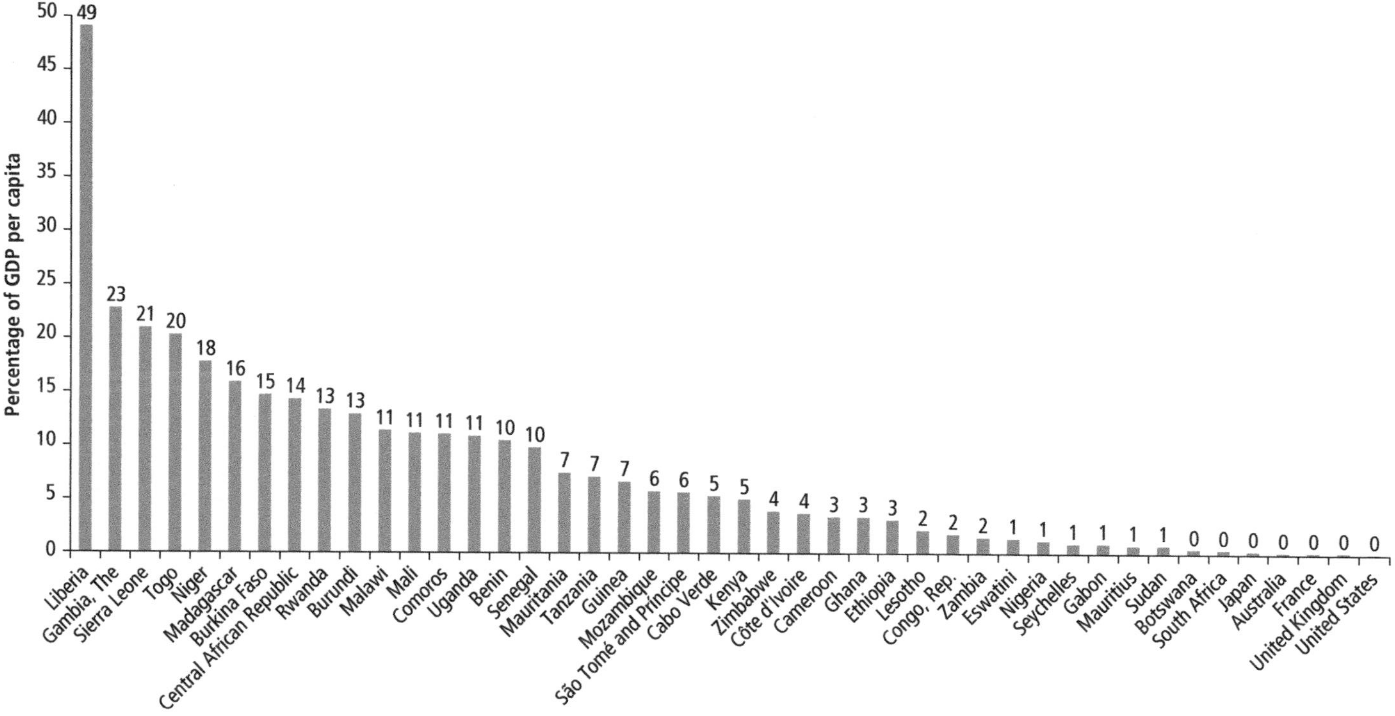

Source: Trimble, Kojima, and Perez Arroyo 2016.
Note: A refrigerator consumes roughly 459 kilowatt hours per year. GDP = gross domestic product.

many countries in Africa remain unaffordable for most households to consume much above the lifeline rate.

Affordability is a key determinant of whether utilities will be able to meet demand and expand access (Kojima and Trimble 2016). Many households cannot afford connection fees and usage tariffs, thereby limiting the expansion of access. Some resort to sharing meters to avoid connection fees, and few can afford subsistence consumption of 30 kilowatt hours a month under current service charges. Sharing and underconsumption constrain utility income, limiting utilities' ability to expand and maintain the electricity network.

Unreliability Is Pervasive Even When Access Is Achieved

Reliability of electricity supply is a major constraint in Africa. The proportion of firms experiencing outages is higher than in any other region (figure 1.7, panel a). A majority of enterprises in the region use generators as a coping strategy for unreliable electricity; this too is a higher proportion of enterprises compared with other regions (figure 1.7, panel b).

Outages have become a characteristic feature of most economies in Africa. Households and firms endure several hours of the day and night without access to power. Even in instances when power is available, brownouts are prevalent, thereby limiting end users' potential utilization of electricity.[3]

Map 1.1 shows the share of firms and households in Africa with access to reliable electricity, using data from the latest rounds of the Enterprise and Afrobarometer surveys.

Map 1.1, panel a, shows the precarious situation facing firms in the region in access to reliable electricity for their activities. In 25 of the 29 countries in Africa shown on the map, fewer than one-third of firms have reliable access to electricity. In other words, more than two-thirds of firms in these countries experience electricity outages, with direct implications for their operations. Firms in Liberia, Namibia, and South Sudan are relatively better off than their counterparts in other countries, with the share of firms with a reliable supply of electricity at 55.7 percent, 73.1 percent, and 84.7 percent, respectively.[4]

Similarly, at the household level (map 1.1, panel b), reliability is a significant concern; the share of households with reliable access is low in many countries. Apart from South Africa, fewer than two-thirds of households in these countries have reliable access to electricity. In Nigeria, Kenya, Mali, and Tanzania, for instance, fewer than a third of households have access to reliable electricity.

The level of reliability experienced by households also varies strongly across the region. Figure 1.8 shows the variation across countries in the reliability of grid electricity. In countries including Ghana, Burundi, Zimbabwe, Uganda, Liberia, Sierra Leone, Nigeria, and Guinea, more than 50 percent of connected

Figure 1.7 Enterprise Electricity Reliability

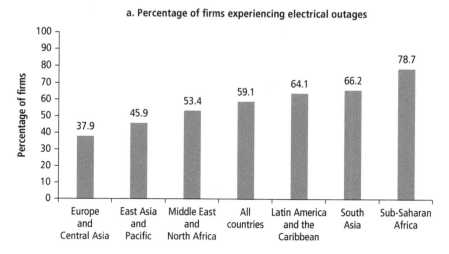

a. Percentage of firms experiencing electrical outages

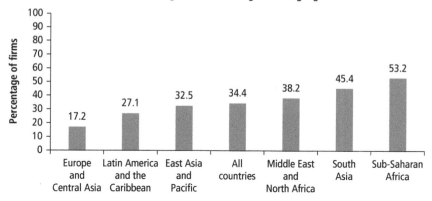

b. Percentage of firms owning or sharing a generator

Source: Enterprise Surveys (http://www.enterprisesurveys.org); World Bank.
Note: Based on surveys carried out during the period 2010–17.

households reported receiving electricity supply not more than 50 percent of the time. By contrast, Cabo Verde, South Africa, Eswatini, Gabon, Côte d'Ivoire, and Mali appear to have relatively reliable electricity supply, with at least 80 percent of households reporting having service at least most of the time. Aside from the prevalence of outages, some households report that despite being connected to the grid, they never received power. For example, in Uganda, Liberia, and Sierra Leone, more than 30 percent of households report never having electricity despite being connected to the grid.

Map 1.1 Access to Reliable Electricity, by Firms and Households

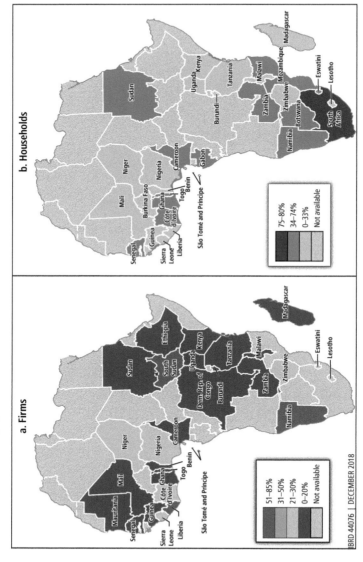

IBRD 44076 | DECEMBER 2018

Sources: Firm data from Enterprise Surveys 2013–17; household data from Afrobarometer surveys 2014/15.
Note: Panel a (firms) is derived from the World Bank Enterprise Surveys data portal that reports the share of responding firms reporting electricity outages. The figure represents the complementary percentage (that is, 100 percent minus the percentage from the portal). Panel b (households) shows the share of households that receive electricity supply most of the time.

Figure 1.8 Reliability of Grid Electricity in Connected Households in Africa

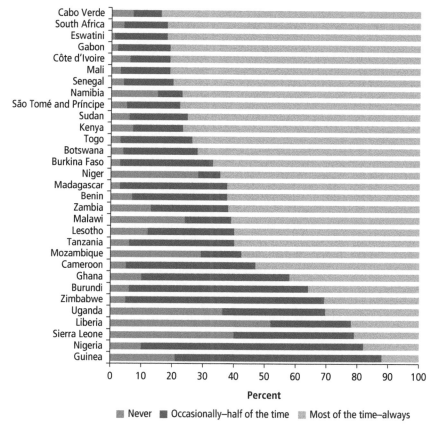

Source: Afrobarometer data 2014/15.

Nigeria is a stark example. The country enjoys a coverage rate of almost 100 percent, which would deceptively imply that it has achieved the goal of universal electrification, at least in the urban areas. However, fewer than 20 percent of households report having electricity at least most of the time. About 51 percent of households report having electricity occasionally in their dwelling. Whether such households should be classified as households with access to electricity remains an open question. The prevalence of brownouts, not captured by the data at hand, became apparent during fieldwork in Nigeria. Often, although the electricity supplied to households might be sufficient to power a lightbulb, the capacity is not enough to power a fan or refrigerator. These issues highlight the importance of the multidimensional measure of electricity access rather than the current binary measure.

Challenges Requiring Sound Strategies

Electricity access in Africa is hindered by the financial capability of utilities to meet supply and the ability of households to pay (Kojima and Trimble 2016). In a well-functioning market, supply and demand converge at a price that satisfies producers and consumers. However, regulatory policies for electricity vary throughout the region, affecting supply. Some countries have separated production and transmission and allow independent power producers; other countries have state-owned monopolies. According to a 2016 report, independent power producers operate in 18 African countries, accounting for 13 percent of the region's total generation capacity, and more countries could consider taking advantage of private sector investment to expand electricity supply (Eberhard et al. 2016). For example, off-grid solutions led by start-ups are growing to meet demand, especially in rural areas; venture capital investment in this segment rose from US\$19 million in 2013 to more than US\$200 million in 2016 (McKibben 2017). Demand is affected by high costs, but poorly targeted subsidies are negatively affecting maintenance and investment (IMF 2013). If electricity markets functioned efficiently and facilitated private investment, more countries could quicken the pace of electrification, as in Ghana, which has enacted some reforms to its electricity sector (World Bank 2017). Fixing this dysfunction of electricity markets will require improving the regulatory environment in most of the poorest performers in Africa facing low electricity access (figure 1.9).

Government Must Foremost Take Leadership with Adequate Planning

Experiences elsewhere indicate that the centerpiece of successful electrification rollout is the preparation and effective implementation in each country of a government-led national electrification strategy addressing in a systematic and coordinated manner the institutional, technical, and financial aspects of electrification. However, according to the latest RISE (Regulatory Indicators for Sustainable Energy) report (2016), 17 out of 35 African countries do not have any officially approved electrification plan. An adequate regulatory framework will be needed to attract investment in all areas of the sector (generation, transmission infrastructure, distribution, and operational management) to fill the gap where public funding falls short.

The private sector is needed to fill the investment gaps. Such investments could also target complementary factors (see chapter 5) that will help translate electrification into rising incomes and jobs. Potential complementary factors include a deepening of the financial sector or enhanced infrastructure, such as roads linking large cities and connecting communities to markets and large urban centers. However, some of those complementary factors may not always

Figure 1.9 Regulatory Indicators for Sustainable Energy (RISE), Bottom 20 Countries Relative to the Highest Performer in Africa, 2016

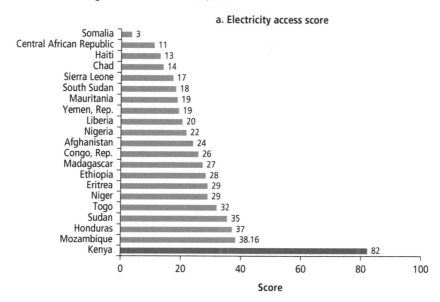

a. Electricity access score

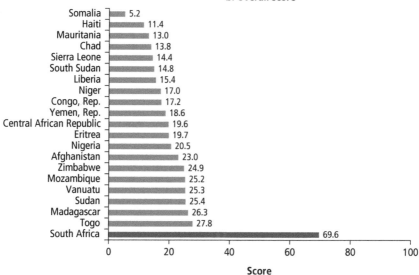

b. Overall score

Source: Banerjee et al. 2017.

be attractive for private investors or might be part of the prerogative of the government. Those areas may include supporting, mechanizing, and modernizing the often large and informal economies, or investing in skills.

Development partners can play a crucial role where needed to help facilitate the interaction between private investors and governments, from providing technical assistance for electrification planning to supporting building up the right regulatory environment, and from providing concessional financing to risk mitigation (for drought, oil price shocks, and conflicts). This concerted effort should lead to falling prices for electricity coupled with rising household incomes, making access more affordable for a more significant share of the population at cost-reflective tariffs that would allow utilities to be financially viable.

Historically, fast progress took strong government commitment and leadership in planning and coordination, as in Vietnam (box 1.1).

BOX 1.1

Accelerating Access to Electricity: Lessons from Vietnam

Vietnam's experience in rural electrification provides some lessons for accelerating the pace of electrification across the continent. The authorities undertook serious planning and coordination, prioritized productive uses of electricity, and ensured funds were available for financing capital costs. Thereafter, all efforts from all stakeholders could be catalyzed through the framework that the government established. Vietnam's success took political commitment to set goals and leadership to plan and then coordinate implementation.

Strong government leadership, careful planning, and coordination. Electricity provision to a significant portion of Vietnam's rural population was rapidly achieved, in large measure because of the unwavering national commitment to rural electrification by the country's political leadership. Government decision makers recognized the high societal demand for access to electricity, and by the early 1990s, electricity access rates had been made a key indicator for the yearly socioeconomic development assessment of every commune, district, and province.

The central government demonstrated its commitment to rural electrification by incorporating it into its 5-year plans and 10-year strategy. In a 1999 policy paper, the Ministry of Industry outlined the objectives and principles to guide the rural electrification process. This guidance provided clear direction for the government's approach, accelerating the program in its initial stages. The allocation of responsibilities for rural electrification was formalized for the first time in the same year, enabling the rural

(continued next page)

BOX 1.1 (continued)

electrification program to be branded as "State and People, Central and Local, Working Together." Government commitment at all levels—central, provincial, and local—was a critical element of Vietnam's rural electrification program.

Prioritizing productive use. The initial focus of Vietnam's electrification program was on promoting productive uses to stimulate the agricultural and industrial sectors. Policy makers prioritized areas with high potential growth in the productive uses of electricity based on the expectation that these areas would be a large source of revenue for the companies involved. Furthermore, productive use of electricity in these areas would translate to higher income, in turn leading to greater electricity consumption and contributing to the financial viability of utilities. This initial focus on areas with potential growth in the productive use of electricity, coupled with the overall economic growth during the *Doi Moi* years, as well as the increased availability of new generation capacity and 500 kilovolt lines, enabled the authorities to gradually shift their focus to steady gain in household electrification (figure B1.1.1).

Figure B1.1.1 Vietnam: Access to Electricity

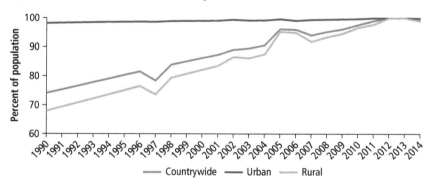

Source: World Bank, World Development Indicators.

Assured funds for financing capital costs. The expansion of rural electric systems in Vietnam relied on multiple sources of financing, including customer contributions; commune, district, province, and central government budgets; special surcharges on urban customers; private investors; borrowing; and retained depreciation from the state utility (Vietnam Electricity, EVN). The cost-sharing approach to financing rural electrification investment was a key factor underlying the rapid expansion of access to electricity to a large proportion of the population. Cost sharing by local communities, in particular, ensured a sense of community ownership and sustained local commitment to the proper operation and maintenance of rural electricity systems.

Keeping Long-Term Development Objectives at the Center of Electrification Efforts

Electricity is a long-term investment, for which the returns may take years or decades to materialize. It took nearly 40 years before the impact of electrification was realized in the United States in growth in manufacturing productivity (figure 1.10, panel a), with about half of total factor productivity growth in the 1920s accounted for by electricity (David 1989). Similar to electricity, investment in computers beginning in the 1970s did not appear to translate into immediate productivity gains. This was noted by economist Robert Solow, who

Figure 1.10 TFP in Manufacturing and Personal Computer Ownership and Business Sector Multifactor Productivity, United States

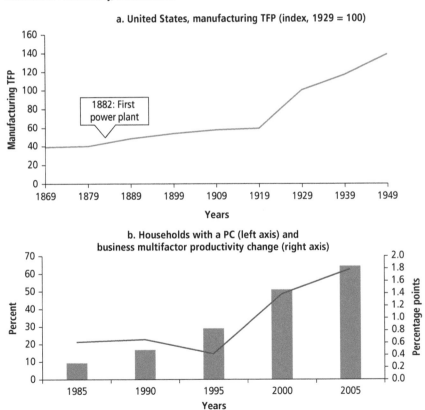

a. United States, manufacturing TFP (index, 1929 = 100)

1882: First power plant

b. Households with a PC (left axis) and business multifactor productivity change (right axis)

■ PC at home ——— Multifactor productivity

Sources: Kendrick 1961; U.S. Census Bureau; Bureau of Labor Statistics.
Note: PC = personal computer; TFP = total factor productivity.

famously said, "You can see the computer age everywhere but in the productivity statistics" (Solow 1987). Productivity increases did not kick in until computers reached a diffusion threshold. U.S. homes with computers, a proxy for overall computerization in the country, reached 50 percent in 2000.

Private business sector multifactor productivity took off, with annual average growth between 1995 and 2005 three times higher than in the preceding five years (figure 1.10, panel b).[5] This rising productivity is largely attributed to greater use of information technology products (Sichel, Oliner, and Stiroh 2007).

Similarly, the full impact of electrification could take time to be realized in Africa. Electricity, along with digital technology, is considered a general-purpose technology (GPT) (Ristuccia and Solomou 2010). Such technologies have a significant impact on economic transformation. Unlike other factors that boost productivity, such as innovation, GPTs take time to sow and time to reap (Helpman and Trajtenberg 1998). GPTs are characterized by a slow diffusion process followed by rapid productivity growth:

> Growth that is driven by general purpose technologies is different from growth driven by incremental innovation. Unlike incremental innovation, GPTs can trigger an uneven growth trajectory, which starts with a prolonged slowdown followed by a fast acceleration. (Helpman 2010, 51)

Could Africa be poised for a significant increase in productivity from electricity? The region is past due for a productivity boom, with its first electricity plants installed more than 100 years ago. The level of electricity access in Africa, 43 percent in 2016, is almost the same as it was in the United States in 1921 when the noticeable growth in manufacturing productivity began. However, electricity-assisted economic transformation in Africa will require greater commercial use of electricity, which is currently constrained by the lowest reliability and highest relative costs compared with other developing regions.[6] These deficits need to be addressed to attract greater business investment in agricultural processing plants, factories, offices, and data centers. Governments can support commercial use through the provision of reliable electricity at competitive prices in export processing zones and industrial and technology parks (Hallward-Driemeier and Nayyar 2018).

Figure 1.11 depicts a framework for thinking about electrification in Africa. Short-run impacts include social benefits, such as lighting for reading, reduced use of combustible fuels, and enhanced security. With electrification, business opportunities become available for micro, small, and medium-size enterprises in areas such as hairdressing, eating establishments, and tailoring. Impacts rise in the medium term as complementary factors are introduced and households and businesses adjust to electricity's potential. Education and health outcomes may improve through the electrification of schools and clinics. Economic impacts grow as electricity becomes increasingly available as a strategic input for industries and services.

Figure 1.11 Thinking Long Term about the Impacts of Electrification in Africa

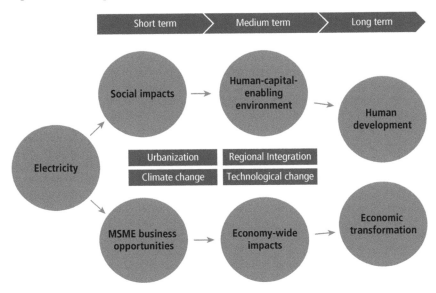

Note: MSME = micro, small, and medium-sized enterprises.

In the long term, this sequence can result in improved human development and the transformation of African economies. In sum, delaying electrification may have a high opportunity cost in terms of the timing of technology adoption and the quality of service delivery, such as health care and education. It may also affect how urbanization unfolds, whether new cities emerge, or existing cities continue to be crowded. Therefore, countries with financial capacity should not delay the rolling out of electrification. And others should rethink their strategies to speed up the progress and impacts of electrification.

Contemporaneous Megatrends Must Not Be Ignored in Planning

Four trends will affect the region's electricity future: urbanization, technological change, regional integration, and climate change. Significant uncertainty surrounds the evolution and timing of these factors, complicating electrification planning in areas such as the appropriate mix of power that balances cost effectiveness with carbon reduction and grid and off-grid solutions.

Urbanization Is Happening Fast, Affecting the Urban-Rural Equation in Planning
By 2040, the forecast is that more than half the population in Africa will be living in urban areas (figure 1.12), which should make it cheaper to provide electricity to more people, given that it is less costly to connect urban areas. However, proactive planning will be necessary to ensure that transmission and

Figure 1.12 **Africa's Urban Population**

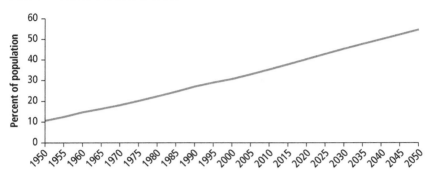

Source: United Nations Department of Economic and Social Affairs 2014.

distribution networks are available before the migration from rural areas occurs. At the same time, achieving greater access to electricity in rural areas may miti-gate urbanization, reducing the flow of people into already overcrowded cities where infrastructure is stretched. Both scenarios, if handled correctly, can be positive developments for Africa.

Early investment in infrastructure, including electrification, can positively shape Africa's cities, which are growing rapidly as people migrate from rural areas. Cities in Africa are projected to increase by 76 million people between 2015 and 2020, and by 2050, they will be home to more than 1 billion residents. Infrastructure needs to be planned to reduce costs and increase efficiency (box 1.2). A recent World Bank report finds that delaying the provision of infra-structure, such as electricity, until after settlement can significantly increase the cost of access and induce the growth of slum communities (Lall, Henderson, and Venables 2017). The report notes that electricity provision is greater the more densely populated a city is and the closer residents are to the central busi-ness district.

A long-term study of settlements in Dar es Salaam, Tanzania, finds that plots where services, including electricity, were installed in advance have higher val-ues than other locations in the city (Regan et al. 2016). It shows empirical evi-dence from Tanzania on strong long-run benefits of the World Bank's Sites and Services Project, in which infrastructure services are provided ahead of the development of urban settlements. The results show high land and property values in areas that benefited from the project relative to comparator areas where infrastructure services were provided after settlement. The latter areas are characterized by disorganized and dysfunctional service provision. High prop-erty values in preplanned communities offer high tax potential, which can be used to finance future investments.

BOX 1.2

What Does Urbanization Mean for Electricity Access?

Urbanization trends in Africa will affect rural and urban electrification efforts. According to a recent World Bank report, "Urban areas in Africa comprise 472 million people. That number will double over the next 25 years as more migrants are pushed to cities from the countryside. The largest cities grow as fast as 4 percent annually" (Lall, Henderson, and Venables 2017, 11). Moreover, the share of Africans living in urban areas is projected to grow from 38 percent in 2015 to 50 percent by 2040, meaning that as urban populations increase, rural population density may decline. As countries strive to meet Sustainable Development Goal 7, universal access to electricity, a stark shift of population from rural to urban areas will have a marked impact on the pace and strategic thrust of electrification efforts.

Increased population density reduces the per capita cost of electrification, increasing its financial viability. The cost of 1 kilometer of electricity distribution line is relatively constant for any given system design, and household consumption is relatively constant as well. Therefore, the financial return of a given stretch of residential distribution line is dependent on the number of connected consumers.[a] As population density increases, financial returns improve, explaining why denser urban populations can be more cost effectively served than rural areas.

To the extent that urbanization results in sparser rural populations, urbanization will make rural electrification less financially attractive and could skew service to off-grid solutions. In areas that are currently served, urbanization could result in reduced revenue from rural consumers. Where new service is needed, per capita capital expenditure could increase. In all cases, sparser populations result in higher operating costs per capita. Sparse populations without electricity, or more widely separated population clusters, tend to favor minigrid or stand-alone systems over grid extension as electricity supply solutions. Hence, urbanization could skew electricity service provision to more off-grid solutions, at least for the initial phases of electrification.

Urbanization increases electricity demand given higher incomes in cities, potentially exacerbating the financial strain on utilities in the region. Urban dwellers tend to have higher per capita electricity consumption than their rural counterparts, which means that urbanization is likely to fuel increased demand for electricity. This can be good for power utilities if they bill and collect for the power used. However, it would not be so good in the frequent cases in which electricity theft is rampant and tariffs are set below the cost of service.[b] In either case, increasing demand creates a need for continuous upgrading and expansion of the supply, transmission, and distribution systems, equating to a continued need for capital investment. Such investment will be manageable if the power utility is financially sound. However, in most countries in Africa, this is not the case (Kojima and Trimble 2016). Hence, rapid urbanization increases the financial strain on the power sector, causing problems.

a. This analysis is simplified, given that it does not account for commercial or industrial users. Frequently, a single "high-consumption" consumer can establish the financial viability of a line extension.
b. Even if the average tariff is set at the cost-recovery level, to the extent that urban slum dwellers are under the "lifeline" (subsidized) tariff threshold, adding new consumers would be a financial loss for the utility.

Electrification can curb rural-urban migration and reduce the growth of slum communities. Evidence from Ethiopia suggests that rural electrification results in a 26 percent reduction in rural-urban migration (Fried and Lagakos 2017). A slower rate of migration could help make the planning of urban electrification more manageable.

Technology Is Changing and Requires Dynamic Thinking

Technological change and innovation in power generation and the appliances that use electricity are ongoing. Considerable research around the world focuses on renewable energy, resulting in lower cost and higher output generation. Appliances are becoming ever more efficient, driven by energy savings standards, and dropping in price. The cost of a solar home system capable of powering a television, radio, lights, and cell phone charging will drop from US$991 in 2009 to US$193 by 2020 (IEG 2016). With cheaper, more powerful off-grid systems, electricity consumption could increase in the region, generating more productive use and financial viability for investors.

Technology and innovation are affecting the electricity sector, just as these trends have affected other sectors of the economy over the past few decades. Their characteristics include the growing use of data generated by networked sensors to monitor systems, and better tailoring of supply to customer behavior. New business models backed by risk-taking investors are disrupting sectors ranging from retail to transportation and have now entered the electricity sector, particularly for off-grid solutions (McKibben 2017). A recent report from the World Economic Forum outlines how distributed storage, advanced metering, and data-driven demand-side management are affecting the electricity network (WEF 2017). The grid is becoming increasingly digitized, with smart meters and sensors and increasing automation. Customers will be at the center of this new model, as both consumers and suppliers (figure 1.13).

Although these changes are initially taking place largely in developed nations, they are already spilling over into Africa. For example, several start-ups are active in the region's off-grid solar market, using innovative pay-as-you-go schemes linked to mobile money and cloud services (McKibben 2017). The systems deploy sensors that allow remote monitoring of electricity consumption (ITU and Cisco 2015). These trends reflect innovation in the region's off-grid development, which could be more effective if it were integrated into an electricity-wide strategy incorporating distributed energy resources. The region can leapfrog by incorporating these technology developments into greenfield deployments.

Regional Integration Can Help Power the Region

Some African countries are energy rich; neighbors getting power from those countries can lower costs, enhance regional cooperation, and improve reliability. There is considerable scope for expanding regional electricity trade. There

Figure 1.13 Future Electricity Network

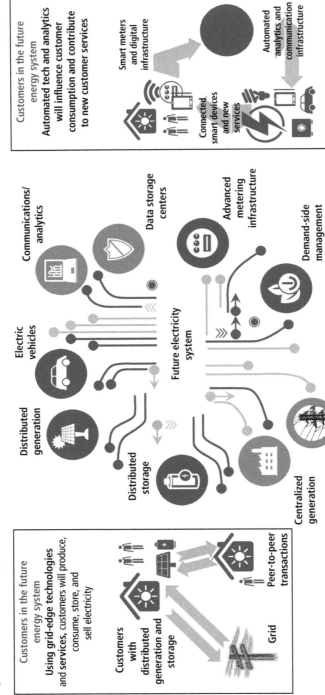

Customers in the future energy system
Automated tech and analytics will influence customer consumption and contribute to new customer services

Smart meters and digital infrastructure

Connected smart devices and new services

Automated analytics and communication infrastructure

Communications/ analytics

Data storage centers

Electric vehicles

Distributed generation

Future electricity system

Advanced metering infrastructure

Demand-side management

Distributed storage

Transmission and distribution

Centralized generation

Customers in the future energy system
Using grid-edge technologies and services, customers will produce, consume, store, and sell electricity

Customers with distributed generation and storage

Peer-to-peer transactions

Grid

Source: WEF 2017.

are 8 net power exporters and 19 net power importers in the region; the remaining countries do not trade power (Trimble, Kojima, and Perez Arroyo 2016). It is estimated that effective implementation of regional power pools could lower power investment costs in Africa by US$80 billion through 2040 (Castellano, Kendall, and Nikomarov 2015).

Regional integration improves economic efficiency and has several benefits (Economic Consulting Associates 2010). These benefits include lower investment requirements as a result of economies of scale (which can also enhance investment interest) and reduced costs from avoided investment on peak capacity. Reliability and energy security are also improved. There are environmental and fiscal benefits such as lower air and water pollution and deforestation and reduced costs for utilities. Implementation of regional power pools increases contact between countries to develop laws and plans, fostering closer political ties and strengthening regulatory, legal, and technical capacity, which is particularly relevant for smaller countries that can leverage the expertise of a wider group. The multilateral framework could also reduce the influence of single-interest groups.

Experiences from East Africa illustrate some of the economic benefits of sharing power. The Eastern Africa Power Pool (EAPP) was created in 2005 and has eight participating countries.[7] EAPP's high-level goal is to facilitate regional integration to help further sustainable development. Specific objectives include increasing energy security; optimizing energy resources; coordinating and cooperating on planning, development, and operation; increasing supply; and facilitating competition in the sector. Key activities include harmonization of energy sector plans, establishing interconnection points, and developing common grid codes. EAPP reckons that regional power pooling could generate a net benefit of up to US$32 billion between 2013 and 2038 (Tesfaye 2011).

Climate Change Calls for Difficult Choices on the Energy Mix

Weather disorders associated with climate change are causing droughts in the region, affecting Africa's vast hydroelectric potential (Cole, Elliott, and Strobl 2014). Zambia has had to ration electricity because water levels in the dams have dropped as a result of lack of rain attributed to climate change (Mfula 2016). At the same time, global commitments to reduce carbon emissions affect power generation decisions. There are various scenarios for the power mix in the region. At this stage, considerable uncertainty surrounds the trade-offs between costs, resiliency, carbon emissions, and consumption and the appropriate power generation source.

Africa has abundant renewable energy resources. More than 90 percent of Africa's economically viable hydropower potential, equivalent to about one-tenth of the world total, is unexploited (Eberhard et al. 2011). However, hydro accounted for just a quarter of installed electricity capacity in the region in 2014 (Trimble, Kojima, and Perez Arroyo 2016). Despite the potential of solar and wind, they accounted for just 3 percent of capacity in 2014.

The climate change issue is contentious, and countries need to determine their energy transition trajectory. Different models will lead to different conclusions driven by assumptions on various parameters that should be set principally by countries themselves. Although there is general agreement about the future level of energy generation in Africa (that is, about 1,000 terawatt hours by 2030), scenarios differ on the mix of sources and costs. The two scenarios discussed below illustrate how divergent conclusions could be reached based on differing assumptions.

Figure 1.14 Africa Power Generation Scenarios

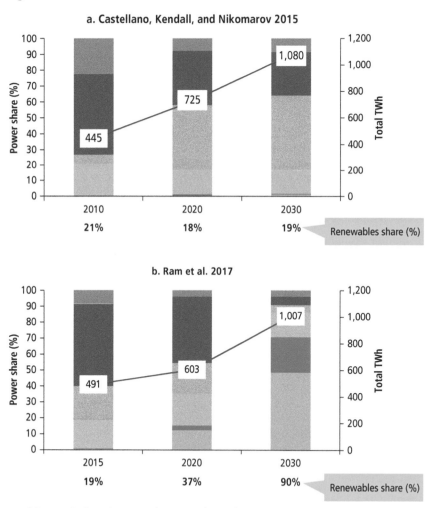

Sources: Adapted from Castellano, Kendall, and Nikomarov 2015 and Ram et al. 2017.
Note: Other includes bioenergy, geothermal, oil, and nuclear. TWh = terawatt hours.

Some continue to see a future dominated by fossil fuels. Gas is especially favored because regional power pools can draw on large reserves in some countries. Castellano, Kendall, and Nikomarov (2015) project a scenario roughly similar to today, driven by gas, coal, and hydropower (figure 1.14, panel a), requiring more than US$800 billion for new generation capacity, transmission, and generation through 2040. The authors acknowledge that their scenario generates greater emissions of carbon dioxide, but a higher proportion of renewables in the mix would drive investment requirements up by almost a third. Renewables constitute one-fifth of electricity generation by 2030 in this scenario, roughly the same proportion as today.

A model developed by German and Finnish researchers finds that electricity generation in Africa can be 100 percent provided by renewables by 2050 and more than 90 percent renewable by 2030 at similar capacity levels as those forecast by other experts (Ram et al. 2017) (figure 1.14, panel b). The researchers argue that solar is the cheapest source of electricity in the region and, except in the tropical rain forests, Africa has widely available and evenly distributed sun throughout the year.

Integrating Both Supply- and Demand-Side Considerations

The electrification efforts in Africa have so far mostly focused on supply issues such as the lack of adequate generation and poor or missing distribution systems. As a result, demand-side constraints have been relatively neglected. For example, even in areas where grid service is available, many households are not connected to the grid. Given that the supply constraints have been eliminated in these areas, much of the lack of connections reflects demand-side constraints. Similarly, in rural areas where stand-alone solar systems are available, only some households have them. Therefore, this report focuses on filling key knowledge gaps in the uptake of electricity.

Conclusion

This report focuses on the central issue of uptake for economic transformation in Africa. It addresses barriers to uptake. It argues that productive use through the provision of reliable electricity and complementary enabling factors is central to speeding up uptake while achieving the ultimate objective of electrification (that is, rising incomes and poverty reduction). The only way to simultaneously address the problems of access, low consumption, unreliability, and financial viability of the utilities is for electricity use to generate higher incomes for households.

Road Map

The rest of the report is organized as follows:

- Chapter 2 elaborates on the extent of the uptake deficit and demand constraints.
- Chapter 3 identifies policy levers that could alleviate the challenges associated with low uptake and addresses the importance of the productive use of electricity.
- Uptake is insufficient to realize the benefits of electricity, and the importance of reliability and complementary factors is discussed in chapters 4 and 5, respectively.
- Chapter 6 spells out policy recommendations for accelerating Africa's electrification and magnifying its social and economic impact.

Notes

1. United Nations website on Sustainable Goal 7 (http://www.un.org/sustainabledeve lopment/energy/).
2. OVO Energy website: "Average electricity prices around the world: $/kWh" (https://www.ovoenergy.com/guides/energy-guides/average-electricity-prices -kwh.html).
3. Energy Today website "Brownouts: What Are They? Are They Bad for Computers?" (https://energytoday.biz/blog/brownouts-what-are-they-what-causes -them-are-they-bad-for-computers).
4. Based on Enterprise Surveys in Liberia (2017), Namibia (2014), and South Sudan (2014).
5. *The Economist,* September 21, 2000.
6. The average cost of an electrical connection was almost 4,000 percent of per capita income in 2017 in Africa, and the perceived reliability and tariff transparency was rated 0.9 on a scale of 0–8 (http://www.doingbusiness.org/data/exploretopics /getting-electricity).
7. Eastern Africa Power Pool website (http://eappool.org/about-eapp/).

References

Banerjee, S. G., F. A. Moreno, J. E. Sinton, T. Primiani, and J. Seong. 2017. *Regulatory Indicators for Sustainable Energy: A Global Scorecard for Policy Makers.* Washington, DC: World Bank.

Castellano, A., A. Kendall, and M. Nikomarov. 2015. *Brighter Africa: The Growth Potential of the Sub-Saharan Electricity Sector.* McKinsey & Company.

Cole, M., R. Elliott, and E. Strobl. 2014. "Climate Change, Hydro-Dependency, and the African Dam Boom." *World Development* 60 (August): 84–96.

David, P. 1989. "Computer and Dynamo: The Modern Productivity Paradox in a Not-Too Distant Mirror." Stanford University, Stanford, CA. https://econpapers.repec.org /paper/wrkwarwec/339.htm.

Eberhard, A., K. Gratwick, E. Morella, and P. Antmann. 2016. *Independent Power Projects in Sub-Saharan Africa: Lessons from Five Key Countries*. Washington, DC: World Bank.

Eberhard, A., O. Rosnes, M. Shkaratan, and H. Vennemo. 2011. *Africa's Power Infrastructure: Investment, Integration, Efficiency*. Washington, DC: World Bank.

Economic Consulting Associates. 2010. *The Potential of Regional Power Sector Integration*. London: Economic Consulting Associates.

Fried, S., and D. Lagakos. 2017. "Rural Electrification, Migration and Structural Transformation: Evidence from Ethiopia." International Growth Centre. https://www.theigc.org/publication /rural-electrification-migration-structural-transformation-evidence-ethiopia/.

Hallward-Driemeier, M., and G. Nayyar. 2018. *Trouble in the Making? The Future of Manufacturing-Led Development*. Washington, DC: World Bank.

Helpman, E. 2010. *The Mystery of Economic Growth*. Cambridge, MA.: Harvard University Press.

Helpman, E., and M. Trajtenberg. 1998. *A Time to Sow and a Time to Reap: Growth Based on General Purpose Technologies*. Cambridge, MA: MIT Press.

IEA (International Energy Agency). 2014. *World Energy Outlook 2014*. Paris: IEA. https://www.iea.org/newsroom/news/2014/november/world-energy-outlook-2014 .html.

IEG (Independent Evaluation Group). 2016. *Reliable and Affordable Off-Grid Electricity Services for the Poor: Lessons from the World Bank Group Experience*. Washington, DC: World Bank.

IMF (International Monetary Fund). 2013. *Energy Subsidy Reform in Sub-Saharan Africa: Experiences and Lessons*. Washington, DC: IMF.

ITU (International Telecommunication Union) and Cisco. 2015. *Harnessing the Internet of Things for Global Development*. Geneva: International Telecommunication Union. https://www.itu.int/pub/S-POL-BROADBAND.15-2015.

Kendrick, J. 1961. *Productivity Trends in the United States*. Princeton, NJ: Princeton University Press.

Kojima, M., and C. Trimble. 2016. *Making Power Affordable for Africa and Viable for Its Utilities*. Washington, DC: World Bank. http://documents.worldbank.org/curated /en/293531475067040608/Making-power-affordable-for-Africa-and-viable-for-its-utilities.

Lall, S. V., J. V. Henderson, and A. J. Venables. 2017. *Africa's Cities: Opening Doors to the World*. Washington, DC: World Bank.

Lemma, A., I. Massa, A. Scott, and D. Willem te Velde. 2016. *What Are the Links between Power, Economic Growth and Job Creation?* London: CDC Group.

McKibben, B. 2017. "The Race to Solar-Power Africa." *The New Yorker*, June 19. http:// www.newyorker.com/magazine/2017/06/26/the-race-to-solar-power-africa.

Mfula, C. 2016. "Zambia to Diversify Generation Mix as Drought Hits Hydropower." *Lusaka Times*, May 16.

Ram, M., D. Bogdanov, A. Aghahosseini, S. Oyewo, A. Gulagi, M. Child, and C. Breyer. 2017. *Global Energy System Based on 100% Renewable Energy–Power Sector*. Berlin: Lappeenranta University of Technology and Energy Watch Group.

Regan, T., D. Nigmatulina, N. Baruah, F. Rauch, and G. Michaels. 2016. Sites and Services and Slum Upgrading in Tanzania. The Annual Bank Conference on Africa: Managing the Challenges and Opportunities of Urbanization in Africa, Oxford, UK, July 13, 2016.

Ristuccia, C. A., and S. Solomou. 2010. *General Purpose Technologies and Economic Growth: Electricity Diffusion in the Manufacturing Sector before WWII*. Cambridge, UK: University of Cambridge. doi:https://doi.org/10.17863/CAM.5549.

Sichel, D., S. Oliner, and K. Stiroh. 2007. "Explaining a Productive Decade." *Brookings Papers on Economic Activity* 2007 (2). https://www.brookings.edu/bpea-articles/explaining-a-productive-decade/.

Solow, R. 1987. "We'd Better Watch Out." *The New York Times*, July 12.

Tesfaye, E. 2011. "Benefits of Integrating into a Regional Power Pool." Presentation at the East Africa Power Industry Convention, Kampala, Uganda, September 9. https://www.esi-africa.com/wp-content/uploads/Ephrem_Tesfaye.pdf.

Trimble, C., M. Kojima, and I. Perez Arroyo. 2016. "Financial Viability of Electricity Sectors in Sub-Saharan Africa: Quasi-Fiscal Deficits and Hidden Costs." Policy Research Working Paper 7788, World Bank, Washington, DC.

United Nations Department of Economic and Social Affairs. 2014. "Electricity and Education: The Benefits, Barriers, and Recommendations for Achieving the Electrification of Primary and Secondary Schools." United Nations Department of Economic and Social Affairs, New York.

WEF (World Economic Forum). 2017. *The Future of Electricity: New Technologies Transforming the Grid Edge*. Cologny, Switzerland: World Economic Forum. http://www.bain.com/Images/WEF_Future_of_Electricity_2017.pdf.

World Bank. 2017. *Regulatory Indicators for Sustainable Energy*. Washington, DC: World Bank.

World Bank and International Energy Agency. 2015. *Sustainable Energy for All 2015: Progress Toward Sustainable Energy*. Washington, DC: World Bank. © World Bank; International Energy Agency. https://openknowledge.worldbank.org/handle/10986/22148. License: CC BY 3.0 IGO.

Chapter 2

Low Uptake: A Challenge or an Opportunity?

Sub-Saharan Africa's (hereafter Africa's or SSA's) low income levels significantly limit affordability for a vast majority of the population, which translates into a low willingness to pay (WTP) for electricity. Estimation of the demand for electricity in Africa is quite challenging because it is highly constrained by supply, lack of accurate data, and idiosyncratic shocks that make predictions difficult (Steinbuks and Foster 2010). The International Energy Agency (IEA) estimates that electricity demand in Africa grew by about 35 percent from 2000 to 2012, without accounting for unmet demand. Demand is expected to continue to grow at about 4 percent per year through 2040 (IEA 2014). Castellano, Kendall, and Nikomarov (2015) use a demand-driven approach to project that by 2040, the demand for electricity will grow fourfold yet the electrification rate will reach only 70 to 80 percent, far from the Sustainable Development Goal set for 2030. Many of the projections appear high because of the low base, assumption of sustained economic growth, and increased population. Irrespective of the demand trajectory, uptake and consumption need to rise, and demand needs to be better understood in the process. The financial viability of the sector in the short, medium, and long terms depends in part on the extent of the level of uptake, consumption, and the WTP. It is therefore important to mobilize existing demand and generate new demand.

Electricity Uptake in Areas under the Grid: Low-Hanging Fruit?

The uptake figures in areas already covered by the grid reveal much room for progress if the demand-related challenges are identified and appropriately addressed. In the 20 countries in Africa with the most recent Living Standards Measurement Study[1] data since 2010, the median uptake rate is 57 percent.[2] Other data sources with different sets of countries indicate higher or lower gaps (46 percent uptake using Demographic and Health Surveys [DHS][3] and 70 percent using the most recent Afrobarometer survey[4]) (box 2.1).

BOX 2.1

Data Sources

In this report, data from the Global Tracking Framework, World Development Indicators (WDI), Living Standards Measurement Study (LSMS), Demographic and Health Surveys (DHS), Afrobarometer, and Multi-Tier Framework (MTF) are intensively used for analysis. In some instances, these sources report different numbers for the same variable of interest (for example, access to electricity). The discrepancies occur for several reasons, including differences in the years of the surveys, countries included for regional aggregations, and methodology adopted in the sampling and measurement of access. For instance, in the Afrobarometer survey, access is defined as the percentage of households connected to the grid, whereas in the WDI, it is the percentage of individuals that have electricity in their homes regardless of the source. Despite the differences in the years of the surveys, the overall correlations between the two sources are very high (figure B2.1.1). The correlation between the two series is 0.84, indicating that although the Afrobarometer access rate is consistently higher than that calculated by the WDI, the analysis in the report would not change if WDI data were used.

The study refers to WDI data as the official access figures in the report. However, for more rigorous analysis of the characteristics of households, Afrobarometer, DHS, and the MTF are used extensively because they include other relevant variables.

Figure B2.1.1 Correlation between Electricity Access Figures from Afrobarometer and World Development Indicators

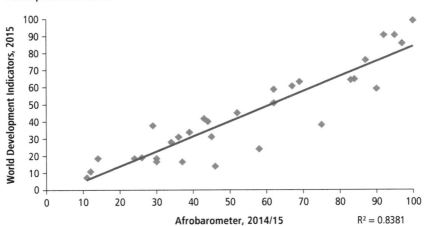

Source: Analysis based on Afrobarometer Round VI, 2014/15 and the 2015 World Development Indicators.
Note: The WDI data (Y-axis) report the share of the population that has access to electricity. The Afrobarometer data (X-axis) report the share of households that have access to electricity.

There are significant variations across and within countries. Uptake is high in a few countries, such as Cameroon, Gabon, Nigeria, and South Africa, and deficient and often below 50 percent in other countries, such as Malawi, Uganda, Niger, Liberia, and Sierra Leone (figure 2.1 and map 2.1, panel a).

Within-country uptake rates vary, with a high concentration around big cities and urban centers. For instance, only the central region of Uganda, which includes the capital, Kampala, has an uptake rate that exceeds 50 percent (map 2.1, panel b).

The many households who live under the electric grid but are not connected raise questions about the demand for electricity and electricity services. These households may also present opportunities to make more rapid progress

Figure 2.1 **Electricity Uptake According to Different Sources**
percent

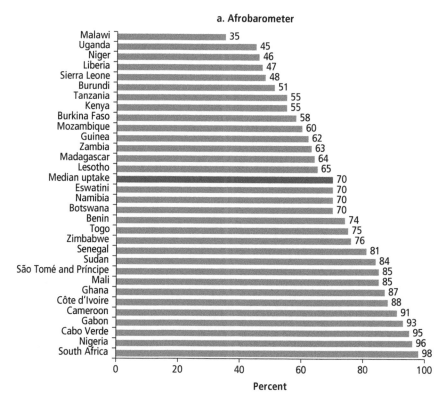

a. Afrobarometer

Country	Percent
Malawi	35
Uganda	45
Niger	46
Liberia	47
Sierra Leone	48
Burundi	51
Tanzania	55
Kenya	55
Burkina Faso	58
Mozambique	60
Guinea	62
Zambia	63
Madagascar	64
Lesotho	65
Median uptake	70
Eswatini	70
Namibia	70
Botswana	70
Benin	74
Togo	75
Zimbabwe	76
Senegal	81
Sudan	84
São Tomé and Príncipe	85
Mali	85
Ghana	87
Côte d'Ivoire	88
Cameroon	91
Gabon	93
Cabo Verde	95
Nigeria	96
South Africa	98

Percent

(continued next page)

Figure 2.1 (continued)

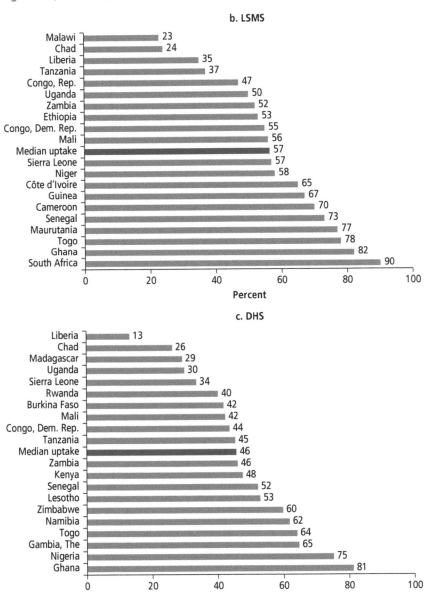

Sources: Adapted from Afrobarometer, LSMS, and DHS.
Note: Uptake refers to households living under the electrical grid that have a connection. DHS = Demographic and Health Surveys; LSMS = Living Standards Measurement Study.

Map 2.1 Electricity Uptake for Households under the Grid

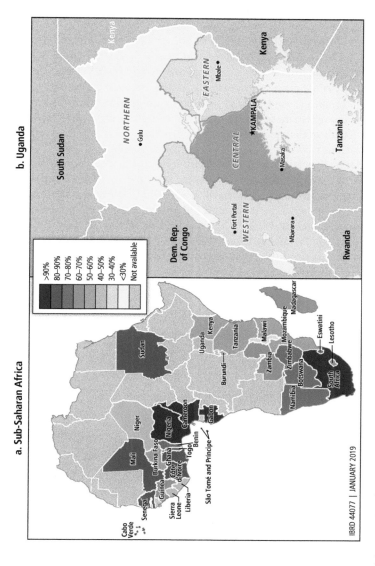

a. Sub-Saharan Africa

b. Uganda

IBRD 44077 | JANUARY 2019

Source: Afrobarometer Round VI 2014/15.
Note: Panel a shows the uptake rate of electricity in 31 countries in Sub-Saharan Africa. The uptake rate is the ratio of households connected to the grid to households living under the grid. Panel b shows the uptake rate across regions in Uganda, which has a national access rate of 24 percent and uptake rate of only 45 percent.

toward universal access if the unconnected could be connected quickly. Although population growth has outpaced access rates over time, the same cannot be said about coverage. Figure 2.2 shows the evolution of access, coverage, and population in 10 African countries where data exist, covering 45 percent of the total population in the region.

It follows from the estimates that if all households that live near the grid were to connect, the average access rate would nearly double for these 10 African countries. Why do households remain unconnected? Does this present an easy opportunity to raise access without necessarily expanding the electric grid, or is it a more complex issue that may worsen as the grid reaches the remaining areas? The answers to these questions are not straightforward and require extensive assessment of demand-related issues, which the rest of this report undertakes in various ways.

The most salient issues in the electricity sector include large investment gaps, inefficient size of countries' power systems, insufficient technical capacity, and poor utility performance (Eberhard et al. 2011). However, addressing the supply-side constraints must go hand in hand with a better understanding of the issues on the demand side. When service becomes available, unless uptake and consumption are high, the sector may not be financially viable. Insufficient uptake and low consumption will also discourage investment in the sector.

Figure 2.3 depicts uptake figures over time in Nigeria, Cameroon, Malawi, Rwanda, and Kenya. The figures are higher in Nigeria and Cameroon but remain below 80 percent. Rwanda and Malawi have shown significant gains

Figure 2.2 Evolution of Coverage, Population, and Access over Time

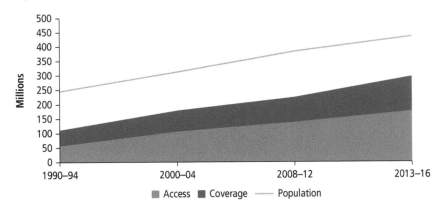

■ Access   ■ Coverage   —— Population

Source: Adapted from Demographic and Health Surveys.
Note: The figure shows the aggregated total population, population living under the grid (coverage), and population connected to the grid (access) in Burkina Faso, Ghana, Kenya, Madagascar, Mali, Nigeria, Rwanda, Tanzania, Uganda, and Zimbabwe. The population of the 10 countries combined accounts for, on average, 45 percent of the total population in Sub-Saharan African countries over the years.

Figure 2.3 Electricity Uptake over Time in Selected Countries

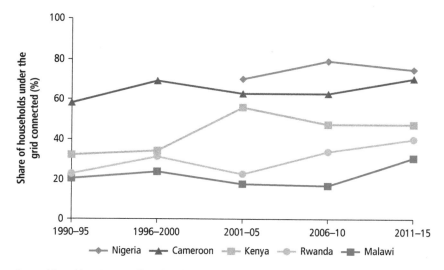

Source: Adapted from Demographic and Health Survey data.

recently from a very low base. Kenya had increases in uptake in the decade before 2005 and a decline afterward. The decline is indicative of the demand-side issues becoming a more significant constraint as the country expanded the grid to more rural and impoverished areas (box 2.2).

Quite a few countries enjoy high coverage rates but uptake rates that are far below 100 percent. Although the differences in coverage among countries point directly to vast differences in infrastructure development, the disparities among uptake rates stress the significance of demand-side barriers to electricity. Different countries fall under various categories in the nexus of demand and supply.

Cabo Verde is the only country with very high coverage and uptake, resulting in more than 90 percent of all households having a grid connection. Eswatini too has high coverage (96 percent), but only 69 percent of all households are connected to the grid, making universal access within reach if demand-related challenges were adequately identified and addressed.

Nigeria, by contrast, has very high uptake rates, with 9 in 10 households under the grid opting for connection. The numbers are also quite high in rural areas, suggesting that supply-side barriers, including generation capacity and extension of infrastructure, are more of a challenge than demand, although electricity theft and bill payments must be addressed. Uptake rates are also high in Guinea, Mali, Mozambique, and Sierra Leone (greater than 80 percent), whereas in Liberia and Malawi, they are low (less than 50 percent).

BOX 2.2

Uptake Rate at a Granular Level in Rural Kenya and Tanzania

Uptake in Rural Kenya

Researchers carried out a comprehensive analysis of electrification in rural Kenya (Lee et al. 2016). Households and businesses within 0.6 kilometer of a transformer in 150 communities in the western part of the country were geo-tagged where there had been capital investments in grid infrastructure over the years. Electrification rates remained very low, including for relatively well-off households, averaging 5.5 and 22.3 percent for households and businesses, respectively. Figure B2.2.1 shows that up to five years following the infrastructure investment, only a small fraction of households and businesses was connected. One of the main reasons was high connection charges (35,000 Kenyan shillings or US$412 at the time of the survey), which might be remedied through subsidies and innovative approaches to financing. At the same time,

Figure B2.2.1 Mean Transformer Community Electrification Rates, by Structure Type and Funding or Installation Year

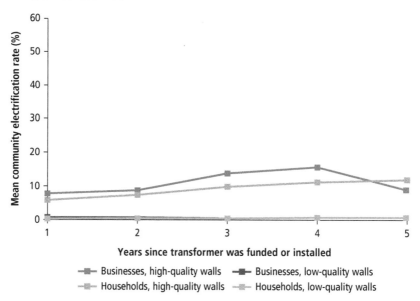

Source: Lee et al. 2016.
Note: Transformer communities are grouped by Rural Electrification Authority project year, which is the fiscal year in which each project was nominated and funded for electrification. Structures with high-quality walls are defined as those made of brick, cement, or stone. Structures with low-quality walls are defined as those of mud, reed, wood, or iron.

(continued next page)

BOX 2.2 (continued)

bureaucratic red tape, low grid reliability, and household credit constraints suppress demand (Lee, Miguel, and Wolfram 2016).

Uptake in Tanzania

The Millennium Challenge Corporation funded a large electrification project in Tanzania between 2008 and 2011. The project, which was implemented by the Tanzanian government, aimed to promote economic inclusion and reduce poverty. The project involved building new lines to the electricity grid and offering low-cost connections to households in a subset of communities getting new lines. Researchers from Mathematica Policy Research assessed the impact of the program in a report published in 2017 (Chaplin et al. 2017). The report finds that although the project increased the number of new connections and connection rate in the communities that received the low-cost connection offers, the project was less successful than planned. The number of new connections was less than a third of what was initially projected. Moreover, conducting a comprehensive and robust analysis, the researchers find that the probability of connection decreased with the household's distance to the nearest electric pole. Figure B2.2.2 shows that the probability of connection decreases sharply for households located more than 30 meters from the nearest pole. The national electricity company imposed a rule that made the connection charge far more expensive for households living outside the 30-meter range.

Figure B2.2.2 Probability of Connection and Distance to the Nearest Electric Pole

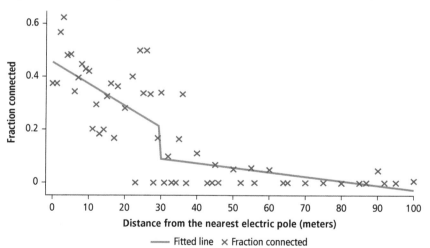

Source: Chaplin et al. 2017.

Low Willingness to Pay Despite High Desire for Access

Studies find a low WTP for access to electricity in African countries, for both grid access and off-grid solutions, especially in rural areas. One study focuses on grid uptake in rural Kenya (Lee, Miguel, and Wolfram 2016). The researchers offered three levels of connection charges to the treatment group in sample households (US$0, US$171, and US$284), and left the control group at US$398, which was the official connection cost at the time. The study found that although uptake was almost universal at zero cost, it was still relatively low at US$171. Uptake increased with lower connection charges but not as sharply as expected. Uptake among households whose housing was characterized as having "high-quality walls" was more than double uptake of those with "low-quality walls." There was also a strong correlation between the revealed preference approach and stated WTP. In 2015, Kenya adopted Last Mile Electrification as a flagship program with financial support from the World Bank and the African Development Bank; the connection fees were reduced to 15,000 Kenyan shillings (US$171).

The World Bank's Multi-Tier Framework (MTF) data allow for further investigation of WTP in African countries. Figure 2.4 reports findings from Rwanda

Figure 2.4 Stated Willingness to Pay for Electricity Services in Rwanda

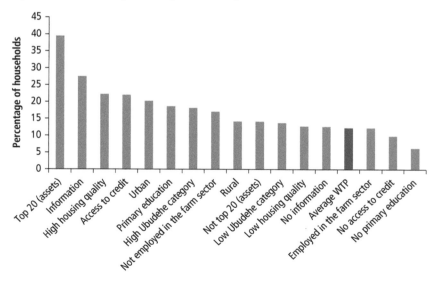

Source: World Bank Multi-Tier Framework data for Rwanda 2017.
Note: Top 20 (assets) refers to the wealthiest 20 percent of households based on an index measuring asset possession. Ubudehe is a term used in Rwanda to classify households in different socioeconomic categories. The higher the category, the more well-off is the household. WTP = willingness to pay.

using the MTF data. Only 12 percent of household heads accepted any of the three options presented. When disaggregating the results by social and economic status using a wide range of variables, uptake was low nearly across the board, with the highest rate among the top 20 percent wealthiest households, whose uptake was 40 percent. This finding is consistent with the experimental results from Grimm et al. (2016) on off-grid lighting solutions in the same country, although those data focus on grid connection rates.

Low WTP does not mean a low desire to access the service. On the contrary, the desire to connect is high among communities. Fieldwork conducted as part of this study in Ethiopia, The Gambia, Nigeria, and Senegal highlights constraints, such as affordability (not only of the connection cost but also of the appliances that will make use of electricity services).

The findings underscore that the WTP numbers may be driven mainly by the ability to pay (that is, low income and credit constraints).

Exploring the determinants of WTP for grid connection requires controlling for a range of factors (education level, wealth status, whether employed in the farm sector, and infrastructure at the community level). Figure 2.5 illustrates

Figure 2.5 Determinants of Willingness to Pay for Electricity Services in Rwanda

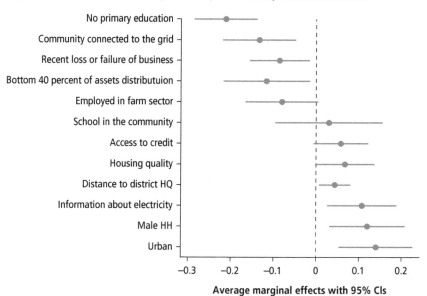

Source: Estimations using World Bank Multi-Tier Framework data for Rwanda 2017.
Note: CI = confidence interval; HH = head of household; HQ = headquarters.

some of the factors of interest. It reports the average marginal effects of a variety of factors on the probability that individuals are willing to accept the connection at a given price. The figure shows that the credit constraint (liquidity), housing quality, and information about electricity affect WTP. Data from Liberia also illustrate this point (box 2.3).

BOX 2.3

Stated Willingness to Pay in Liberia and Zambia

The "stated" willingness to pay (WTP) for a grid connection in Liberia is estimated using Multi-Tier Framework data. WTP offers insight into the role of connection charges in spurring uptake of electricity. Six different connection fees (US$54, US$38, US$31, US$23, US$16, and US$8) were randomly assigned to households. These prices were established in relation to the official connection cost for electricity estimated to be US$54 (Banerjee et al. 2017). Thus, households were randomly offered different levels of connection subsidies ranging from 0 to 100 percent.

Liquidity constraints are known to be a major obstacle to a household's WTP for amenities such as electricity (Greenstone and Jack 2015). To examine the extent to which relaxing credit constraints influences WTP and uptake, households were offered four payment options (100 percent up-front fee, 3-month installment, 6-month installment, and 12-month installment).

Results of the WTP calculations are shown in (figure B2.3.1). At the official connection cost of US$54, uptake ranges between 10 percent (paying the full up-front fee) and 15 percent (12-month installment). Interestingly, even at a 100 percent subsidy (zero connection fees) uptake of electricity is less than 100 percent. This, however, does not imply that the 9 percent of households that declined the offer of connection do not value electricity. Rather, the official connection cost does not represent the full cost. The price of wiring constitutes a large share of the total connection cost and often depends on the size and quality of the housing infrastructure. Indeed, more than 90 percent of households in the survey that declined the offer of electricity connection attributed their decision to their inability to afford the cost of wiring. This result highlights the need for policies aimed at expanding connection to not only focus on official connection fees but also to consider strategies that reduce wiring costs and other nonmonetary constraints to connecting.

Furthermore, payment flexibility appears to matter less with high connection fees. For instance, at a connection fee of US$16, offering a 6-month payment scheme increases uptake by 15 percent. However, uptake increases by only 7 percent at a connection fee of US$38, even with the 6-month payment scheme.

Similar data from Zambia (figure B2.3.2) show qualitatively equivalent findings, that is, an overall low average WTP.

(continued next page)

BOX 2.3 (continued)

Figure B2.3.1 **Stated Willingness to Pay for Grid Electricity in Liberia**

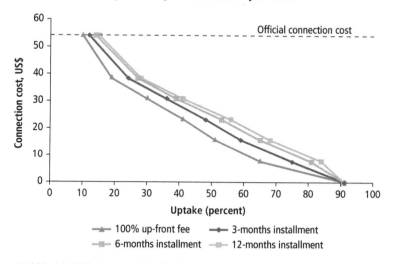

Source: World Bank Multi-Tier Framework data for Liberia 2017.

Figure B2.3.2 **Stated Willingness to Pay for Grid Electricity in Zambia**

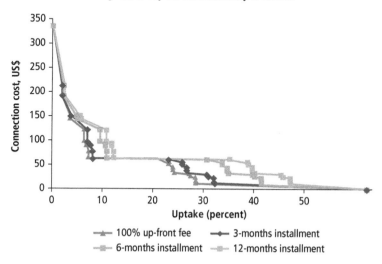

Source: World Bank Multi-Tier Framework data for Zambia 2018.

Demand and Supply Are Interlinked, but Demand Matters More Than Perceived

Both supply- and demand-side considerations affect the electricity access deficit in Africa. Although the demand-side issues are less studied in the literature, acknowledgment of the issues is not new. Separating the supply issues sharply from demand-related issues is not straightforward. To address this challenge, Foster and Caridad Araujo (2004) use a statistical decomposition, as part of a study on infrastructure and poverty in Guatemala, to assess the extent to which the electricity access rate stems from demand only, supply only, or mixed supply-demand constraints. The assumption was that unconnected households living in an area covered by electricity infrastructure could not lack connection because of a supply-side barrier.[5] Conversely, it could be assumed that in areas without the electric grid, the lack of a connection is primarily supply driven.

However, this approach assumes that supply constraints are not a factor in areas under the grid, which is not always correct, because a household under the grid may still live far from the nearest electric pole, or reliability issues may make electricity undesirable even for households that live under the grid. As part of the World Bank's Africa Infrastructure Country Diagnostic Study, Wodon et al. (2009) augment the methodology with an econometric model. They predict uptake using DHS data from 32 African countries to separate the relative share of supply- or demand-side issues. They find that demand constraints may explain up to 52 percent of the electricity access gaps in Africa.[6]

Figure 2.6 reports the results from the application of this methodology to 31 African countries,[7] using newly available data and an array of variables that may explain household uptake (Blimpo, Postepska, and Xu 2018). Demand-related factors could account for 37 percent of the gap in access under conservative assumptions.[8] As would be expected, in rural areas, the supply-side gap dominates (42 percent relative to 32 percent for the demand gap). By contrast, in urban areas, 70 percent of the deficit in access is attributed to demand-side factors. The analysis highlights the divergence across the region in factors explaining the electricity access gap. Central Africa is the most affected by demand-side constraints, which represent 80 percent of the access gap, followed by Southern, West, and East Africa, respectively. Once again, the analysis underscores the need to identify demand constraints and try to relax them. However, this is only the first step toward the end goal; the next step will be for connected households to use more energy than the current levels.

The relative importance of demand and supply constraints varies across countries. The limited sample size does not allow for precise estimation by country, but figure 2.6 shows the results of conducting the same exercise for subgroups of countries. The demand constraints are more pronounced in the Central Africa region and less so in East Africa. As income level rises, demand considerations increase, most likely because countries can expand the grid to more deprived areas. Demand for electricity is also growing even in deprived areas because of high penetration of information and communication technologies, especially the cell phone (box 2.4). Demand considerations account for 56 percent of the overall constraint in lower-middle-income countries, compared with 30 percent in low-income countries. Finally, demand accounts for much of the gap in urban areas (70 percent) relative to rural areas (32 percent).

Figure 2.6 Decomposition of the Access Gap, by Region

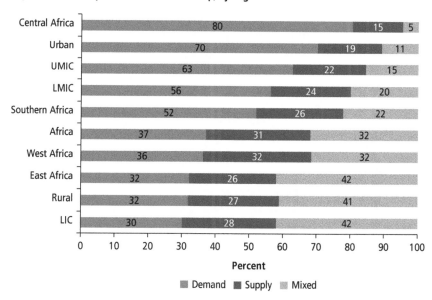

Source: Calculations using Afrobarometer data and adapted from Blimpo, Postepska, and Xu 2018.
Note: LIC = low-income countries; LMIC = lower-middle-income countries; UMIC = upper-middle-income countries.

BOX 2.4

Mobilizing Demand

High cell phone penetration in African countries, including in rural areas, is an indication of the potential for high uptake of electricity and of existing demand. Mobile phones need electricity for recharging, yet there is a far higher level of cell phone possession in rural Sub-Saharan African homes compared with the availability of electricity (see figure B2.4.1). On average, 59 percent of rural households have mobile phones,

(continued next page)

BOX 2.4 (continued)

Figure B2.4.1 Electricity Access and Mobile Phone Ownership, Rural Households in Sub-Saharan Africa, 2016 or Latest Data Available

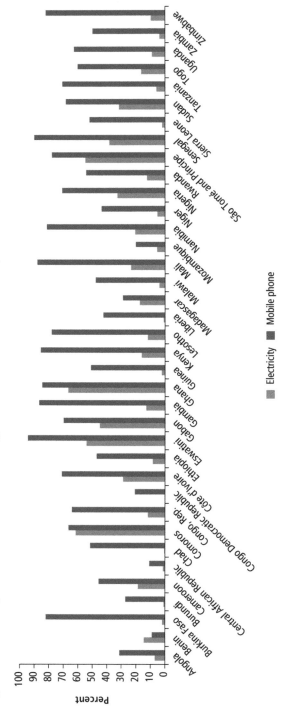

■ Electricity ■ Mobile phone

Sources: Demographic and Health Surveys; Multiple Cluster Indicator Surveys.

(continued next page)

BOX 2.4 (continued)

compared to just 17 percent with electricity. Benin is the only country where the level of rural households with electricity is higher than the level with mobile phones.

Mobile phones need to be recharged, and off-grid households are finding ways of doing so. Users are spending, on average, US$9.60 per year charging cell phone batteries outside their homes, compared with an average cost of just US$1.25 if they had electricity (figure B2.4.2, panel a). It has been estimated that US$2.4 billion was spent in Africa in 2014 for off-grid mobile phone charging. Households spend an even higher amount on kerosene and candles for off-grid lighting (figure B2.4.2, panel b). The US$17 billion spent on off-grid lighting and cell phone charging is roughly equivalent to annual investment in electricity in Africa.

Figure B2.4.2 Annual Cost of Charging Mobile Phones and Distribution of Off-Grid Lighting and Mobile Phone Charging Costs

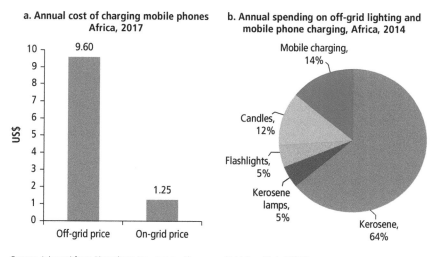

Source: Adapted from Bloomberg New Energy Finance and Lighting Global 2016.

Conclusion

To make electricity expansion financially viable and to provide incentives for private sector participation in the sector, uptake rates need to be higher, and consumption needs to rise as well. Demand constraints must be essential considerations for electrification strategies in the region. These issues are growing in importance as grid expansion or off-grid solar solutions reach more rural and deprived areas. Efforts to reduce connection charges or introduce smart metering have indirectly addressed some of the issues in the past. However, a proactive and concerted effort is needed to understand and circumvent critical constraints. A significant share of unconnected households living under the electricity grid means that much progress could be made toward universal access in those areas without necessarily undertaking the massive infrastructure investment needed to expand the grid. The decomposition exercise in this chapter suggests that in some countries, demand-side considerations take prominence relative to lack of supply. The next chapter identifies and analyzes these constraints.

Notes

1. Living Standards Measurement Studies are household surveys conducted by the World Bank. See http://go.worldbank.org/IPLXWMCNJ0.
2. The uptake rate is calculated based on an analysis of survey micro data. It assumes that if a household has electricity, then all the other households in the enumeration area are within range of the grid. The uptake rate is defined as the proportion of those living under the grid with an electrical connection.
3. Demographic and Health Surveys are household surveys supported by the U.S. Agency for International Development. The surveys are typically conducted in collaboration with national statistical agencies and health ministries. See https://dhsprogram.com.
4. Afrobarometer conducts a range of opinion surveys across the region. It collected information about electricity access in its 2014/15 survey round of 54,000 interviews in 36 African countries. See http://afrobarometer.org/publications/ad75-unreliable-electricity-supply-still-plague-majority-of-africans.
5. See the World Bank's Doing Business website (http://www.doingbusiness.org/en/data/exploretopics/getting-electricity).
6. However, the study defined demand-side constraints solely based on income quintiles, using an index based on the possession of household durables as a proxy.
7. Benin, Botswana, Burkina Faso, Burundi, Cabo Verde, Cameroon, Côte d'Ivoire, Eswatini, Gabon, Ghana, Guinea, Kenya, Lesotho, Liberia, Madagascar, Malawi, Mali, Mozambique, Namibia, Niger, Nigeria, São Tomé and Príncipe, Senegal, Sierra Leone, South Africa, Sudan, Tanzania, Togo, Uganda, Zambia, and Zimbabwe.
8. The decomposition assumes that 10 percent of the deficit in areas that are covered by the grid is still due to supply-related issues, such as households living unreasonably far from the nearest electric pole. It also assumes that if the grid were expanded today to the areas off grid, the uptake would be two-thirds of the current uptake rate in the areas covered.

References

Banerjee, S. G., F. A. Moreno, J. E. Sinton, T. Primiani, and J. Seong. 2017. *Regulatory Indicators for Sustainable Energy: A Global Scorecard for Policy Makers*. Washington, DC: World Bank Group.

Blimpo, M. P., A. Postepska, and Y. Xu. 2018. "Why Is Household Electricity Uptake Low in Sub-Saharan Africa?" Working Paper, World Bank, Washington, DC.

Bloomberg New Energy Finance and Lighting Global. 2016. *Off-Grid Solar Market Trends Report*. Washington, DC: World Bank. https://www.esmap.org/node/71032.

Castellano, A., A. Kendall, and M. Nikomarov. 2015. *Brighter Africa: The Growth Potential of the Sub-Saharan Electricity Sector*. McKinsey & Company.

Chaplin, D., A. Mamun, A. Protik, J. Schurrer, D. Vohra, K. Bos, H. Burak, L. Meyer, A. Dumitrescu, C. Ksoll, and T. Cook. 2017. "Grid Electricity Expansion in Tanzania by MCC: Findings from a Rigorous Impact Evaluation." Millennium Challenge Corporation, Princeton, NJ.

Eberhard, A., O. Rosnes, M. Shkaratan, and H. Vennemo. 2011. *Africa's Power Infrastructure: Investment, Integration, Efficiency*. Washington, DC: World Bank.

Foster, V., and M. Caridad Araujo. 2004. "Does Infrastructure Reform Work for the Poor? A Case Study from Guatemala." Policy Research Working Paper 3185, World Bank, Washington, DC.

Greenstone, M., and K. B. Jack. 2015. "Envirodevonomics: A Research Agenda for an Emerging Field." *Journal of Economic Literature* 53 (1): 5–42.

Grimm, M., A. Munyehirwe, J. Peters, and M. Sievert. 2016. "A First Step Up the Energy Ladder? Low Cost Solar Kits and Household's Welfare in Rural Rwanda." Policy Research Working Paper 7859, World Bank, Washington, DC. https://openknowledge.worldbank.org/handle/10986/25304.

IEA (International Energy Agency). 2014. *Outlook, Africa Energy: A Focus on Energy Prospects in Sub-Saharan Africa*. Paris: International Energy Agency.

Lee, K., E. Brewer, C. Christiano, F. Meyo, E. Miguel, M. Podolsky, H. Rosa, and C. Wolfram. 2016. "Barriers to Electrification for 'Under Grid' Households in Rural Kenya." *Development Engineering* 1 (Supplement C): 26–35.

Lee, K., E. Miguel, and C. Wolfram. 2016. "Experimental Evidence on the Demand for and Costs of Rural Electrification." Working Paper 22292, National Bureau of Economic Research, Cambridge, MA.

Steinbuks, J., and V. Foster. 2010. "When Do Firms Generate? Evidence on In-House Electricity Supply in Africa." *Energy Economics* 32 (3): 505–14.

Wodon, Q. T., S. G. Banerjee, A. B. Diallo, and V. Foster. 2009. "Is Low Coverage of Modern Infrastructure Services in African Cities Due to Lack of Demand or Lack of Supply?" Policy Research Working Paper 4881, World Bank, Washington, DC. http://documents.worldbank.org/curated/en/171921468010246258/pdf/WPS4881.pdf.

Chapter 3

Enabling Higher Uptake: Constraints and Opportunities

Faster progress toward universal access to electricity in Sub-Saharan African (hereafter African or SSA) countries will require identifying constraints and policy levers that affect uptake,[1] affordability, willingness to pay, and consumption. These issues are essential in areas that are covered by the electrical grid and areas that are off the grid. Framing the demand for electricity in Africa from the standpoint of basic consumer theory suggests that consumers would typically choose a bundle of goods and services from all the available options, such that they would receive *maximum expected benefit* from it. These choices are constrained by the household's budget and the prevailing prices of various goods and services (von Neumann and Morgenstern 1944). From the theoretical standpoint, a straightforward implication is that to spur progress toward universal access, electricity needs to be made available and affordable, but it must also yield significant benefits to households relative to their other competing needs and wants.

However, issues of sunk costs and proper consideration of opportunity costs, which may all be present in the context of demand for electricity, create deviations from standard theory, leaving empirical questions (Thaler 1980). For example, several studies suggest that households spend a significant share of their income on alternative sources of energy when, in many cases, that amount could afford them access to modern and more efficient energy (Bacon, Bhattacharya, and Kojima 2010). It is also possible that these various sources serve different purposes for the household, and electricity alone may not fully substitute for them.

This chapter primarily investigates demand-related issues. However, concerted efforts on the supply and demand sides alike will be required to achieve the massive undertaking of universal access. In most African countries, the income levels of poor households are too low for them to afford meaningful electricity consumption, even at lifeline tariff levels, let alone at cost-reflective prices.

Therefore, electricity access must be considered within a broader effort of productivity and job creation so that higher uptake and consumption feed into rising household income.

Additionally, electricity is not a final consumer product but merely an intermediate input or vehicle to desired services. In addition to lighting, access to electricity services would require the acquisition of appliances, which are often quite expensive relative to a household's income. Therefore, when thinking about electricity access, the inevitable question is whether these are simultaneous decisions made by households, or whether they would connect first and later acquire the desired appliances. A sensible approach to thinking about demand and access will not only require prices to decrease; it will also require uptake and consumption to rise and energy to contribute to enabling households to raise their productivity and income through simultaneous access to complementary inputs (for example, access to productive appliances).[2]

Macro Influences on Uptake and Consumption

A basic assessment of demand and supply issues would indicate that faster progress will require prices to come down and household incomes to increase. The effort will include getting more people currently under the grid to connect (densification) and making electricity available to areas currently not covered by the grid (extensification). Analysis of data from several sources indicates that cross-country variation in uptake rates is tightly linked to urbanization, population density, development of industry, and the degree of reliability of the service (table 3.1). The importance of urbanization for uptake should be considered broadly in the overall future electrification strategies of the region.

Table 3.1 **Factors Affecting Uptake and Consumption**

Indicator	Uptake	Consumption
Log GNI		+++
Urban population	+++	+++
Population density	+	+++
Value added in agriculture		
Value added in services	+++	
Governance index	+++	++
Reliability	+	

Sources: Afrobarometer 2014; World Development Indicators 1990–2016; World Energy Statistics 2015.
Note: The Governance Index (Mo Ibrahim Index) is used to analyze uptake while government effectiveness data from the Worldwide Governance Indicators are used to analyze consumption. There are 31 countries for the uptake analysis and 24 for consumption. GNI = gross national income. +, ++, +++ stand, respectively, for statistical significance at the 10 percent, 5 percent, and 1 percent levels.

Figure 3.1 Electricity Consumption and Urbanization

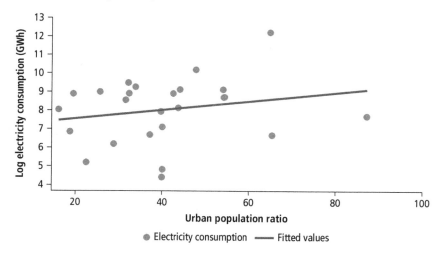

Source: World Energy Statistics 2015.
Note: GWh = gigawatt hours.

Figure 3.1 shows the relationship between electricity consumption and urbanization. A recent regional study highlights the challenges facing African cities, where infrastructure is not keeping up with rapid population growth (Lall, Henderson, and Venables 2017). African urbanization appears to be atypical compared with historical evidence for other regions, with potentially significant implications for Africa's electrification strategies, which, in turn, feeds back into how urbanization unfolds.

Compared with other developing regions of the world, total annual electricity consumption has remained very low in Africa for the past 25 years. Africa is also the only region where a higher share of energy consumption goes to industries relative to households (figure 3.2). From the latest data (2015), in developing Asia, household consumption accounts for 64 percent and industry for 20 percent, compared with Africa, where industry accounts for 54 percent and households only 29 percent.

What Drives Uptake for Areas under the Grid?

Many factors affect the demand for and use of electricity. Low levels of willingness to pay for electricity access, low levels of income, irregular income flows, poor housing quality, and the reliability of the electricity service are all factors that have been identified as affecting uptake and consumption (Blimpo, Postepska and

Figure 3.2 Electricity Consumption, by Sector

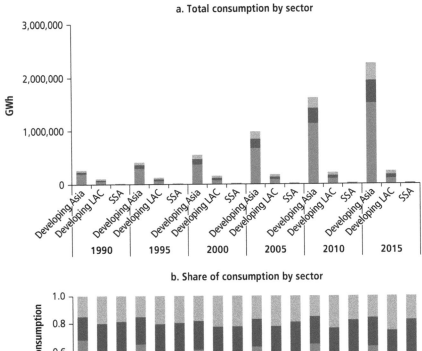

a. Total consumption by sector

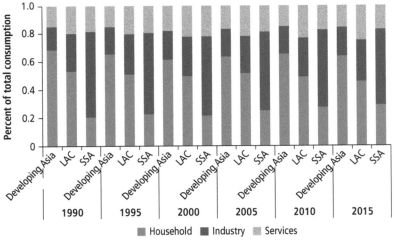

b. Share of consumption by sector

■ Household ■ Industry ▨ Services

Source: World Energy Statistics, 1990–2015.
Note: Consumption is weighted by the population of each country in the region. Developing Asia includes 11 countries (Cambodia, China, India, Indonesia, Lao PDR, Malaysia, Nepal, Philippines, Sri Lanka, Thailand, Vietnam). Latin America and the Caribbean (LAC) includes 18 countries (Argentina, Bolivia, Brazil, Colombia, Costa Rica, Cuba, the Dominican Republic, Ecuador, Guatemala, Honduras, Jamaica, Mexico, Nicaragua, Panama, Peru, Paraguay, El Salvador, and República Bolivariana de Venezuela). GWh = gigawatt hours;

Xu 2018). Additionally, recent studies have paid particular attention to connection charges, analyzing them from the standpoint of the utility as well as households (Blimpo, McRae, and Steinbuks 2018; Blimpo et al. 2018).

Connection Charges: A Critical Entry Point Barrier

Connection charges are the fixed, upfront amount that new customers pay to connect to the distribution network. Golumbeanu and Barnes (2013) discuss and show the relationship between low electrification rates and high connection charges. To understand this key barrier to access, especially for the poor, Blimpo et al. (2018) document facts about the connection process and cost for a few recently connected households in 10 African countries (Cameroon, Côte d'Ivoire, Ethiopia, Gabon, Ghana, Niger, Nigeria, Rwanda, Togo, and Zimbabwe). They focus on households that recently gained access (within a year for the most part) and include interviews with service providers. Four key findings emerged that are relevant to policies that could spur uptake, as described in the following discussion.

The Connection Process Is Often Daunting

The connection requirements and process are often standardized and not designed to alleviate the constraints that the poor face. Figure 3.3 presents the standard steps required to secure a connection. These steps are roughly similar in most of the 10 countries that were surveyed in the study. The first stage for a prospective household is to visit the local office of the utility company to apply for a connection. Sometimes an application fee is required, which varies across countries but is often minimal, ranging between US$1.75 (in Ethiopia) and

Figure 3.3 Process to Get Connected to the Grid

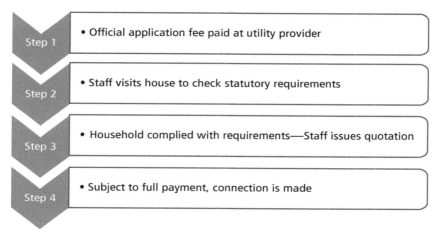

Step 1
- Official application fee paid at utility provider

Step 2
- Staff visits house to check statutory requirements

Step 3
- Household complied with requirements—Staff issues quotation

Step 4
- Subject to full payment, connection is made

US$2.65 (in Togo). However, in some countries, the application fee is waived or bundled with other charges. Hence, there is no explicitly defined cost of application, as in Gabon, where households do not have to pay for the application.

On receipt of the application fee by the utility provider, the technical staff makes an appointment with the household to check the statutory requirements, such as local infrastructure, electrical wiring, and so forth (Step 2). Based on this initial check, a household that complies with all the requirements receives a quotation for cost and, subject to full payment, the grid connection is made. A household that does not pass the inspection check is given the opportunity to make the required changes and book another inspection. Compliance is often a primary source of delay in getting electricity because households may require significant investment to improve their housing quality or rewire the house to meet the utility's minimum requirements.

Many of the surveyed households identified such delays as a significant barrier to access. As illustrated in figure 3.4, the waiting time varies by country. Whereas it took an average of 4 weeks in Cameroon, it took an average of 64 weeks for the Ethiopian households that were interviewed. Figure 3.4 also compares household connection waiting times with corresponding estimates for firms using data from the 2018 World Bank *Doing Business* survey. In Ethiopia and Rwanda, the waiting time for households is about five times the waiting time for firms. This gap may be attributed to policies that seek to reduce the cost of doing business for firms in the respective countries.

Figure 3.4 **Average Number of Weeks to Get Connected to Electricity**

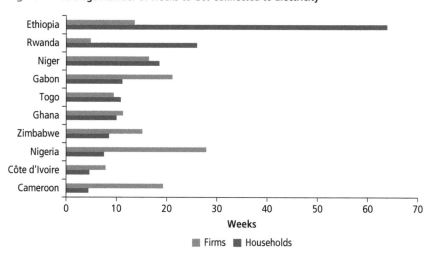

Sources: Adapted from Blimpo et al. 2018 and based on a survey of selected households that connected to the electric grid within a year of the survey date in 10 African countries.

Connection Charges Are Often Too High for Most Households

As is often pointed out in the literature, connection charges are, on average, high relative to the level of income in most countries. The costs range from US$78 in Rwanda and US$148 in Ethiopia, to as high as US$824 in Zimbabwe and US$1,303 in Gabon for a typical household living within a 30-meter radius of the nearest pole (figure 3.5, panel a). For households outside of this radius, the cost is even higher because they must purchase extra electric poles before the

Figure 3.5 Household Connection Costs

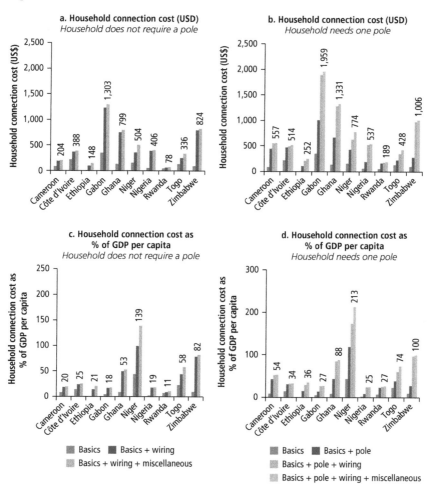

Source: Calculations adapted from Blimpo et al. 2018.
Note: GDP = gross domestic product.

grid can be extended to the house (figure 3.5, panel b). The cost of the electric poles is nontrivial, ranging from US$92 in Togo to US$656 in Gabon. The total cost of connection is mainly driven by the costs of the electric meter and poles. The initial density and distribution of electrical poles in the community significantly affect households' average cost of connection. Municipal policies concerning public lighting could reduce the costs by reducing the average distance to the nearest pole for households, and such policies would have a positive effect on reducing crime and encouraging more economic activity at night.

Total Connection Charges Are Not Fixed and Are Inherently Regressive

Although the cost of connection is often thought of as fixed, it can vary significantly across households within the same country. The variation tends to be regressive, thus exacerbating affordability for the poor. In some cases, it is not only the distance to the pole that matters in determining the cost. For example, in Niger, aside from the distance to the nearest pole, if the house is not aligned straight relative to the lineup of the existing electric poles, the cost may increase significantly (box 3.1). The relatively high cost of electric poles indicates that connection costs are regressive because low-income households, which often live in rural areas where settlement patterns are scattered and less dense, are faced with higher costs. Such households are more likely to have inadequate housing quality and spend a greater share of their income on improving the quality of their housing to meet the minimum requirements of the utility companies.

BOX 3.1

Household Connection Cost: An Illustration from Niger

In Niger, households seeking an electricity connection must submit a request to the utility provider, NIGELEC. There are two types of connection:

- *Connection with extension.* This type of connection is mostly for those whose houses are located very far from a pole. To establish an electrical connection, the installation of a pole is necessary. The number of poles required depends largely on the distance from the house to the nearest existing pole. The cost varies from 500,000 CFA francs ([CFAF]; US$900) to CFAF 5,000,000 (US$9,000).

- *Simple connection.* Households requesting a simple connection should already have a pole near the house. The implication is that such households would not be required to purchase a pole. If the pole is in front of the house and on the same alignment, the cost of the connection is CFAF 60,000 (approximately US$108). However, if the pole is not in the same alignment as the house, the connection cost is nearly double, at CFAF 100,000 (US$180). Thus, it is not sufficient to have a pole near the house; it must also be on the exact alignment as the house.

Strategies to lower these costs, especially the burden of the cost of electric poles, include encouraging coordination among households during the connection process to deal with the externalities associated with the placement of electric poles in each area. The Rwandan government is using some of these types of policies in its strategy for universal access to electricity by 2020,[3] including offering discounts to rural households that organize themselves in a group. Cross-subsidies may also be a workable strategy for reducing the cost per meter for low-income households. For example, in Gabon, household connection costs (excluding the cost of a pole) differ depending on the type of meter bought. For low-income households, the price of the meter is about US$144. For households requesting a single-phase meter, the price rises to US$252, while those requesting three-phase meters could pay a significant amount, up to US$900.

Unofficial Payments Are a Small Proportion of Total Connection Costs
Hidden costs, such as unofficial payments (for example, bribes), are often reported in the provision of various public services in many African countries. In Blimpo et al. (2018), such costs were about 3 percent of total connection costs. These payments were reported in all the countries in the study.

Income Flow and Housing Quality
An exploratory analysis revealed several factors that are consistently associated with higher uptake. The factors that stood out include the level of household income, predictability or variation in household income flow, and housing quality. The analysis controlled for a range of factors at the community and household levels. Qualitative work corroborates the empirical findings, which are described in the following subsections.

Beyond the Level of Income, Income Flow Plays a Role
The level of household income is a consistently significant predictor of uptake. However, not only is the average level of income important, its flow and predictability also correlate with households' willingness to connect to electricity services. A recurring payment of even a small amount can present a major challenge for households that generate their income on an irregular basis. Smart metering and ready boards play crucial roles in overcoming this constraint. However, only the creation and enhancement of income-generating activities can increase uptake and enable households and businesses (income generation), government (through taxes), and utilities (via revenues) to overcome financial constraints in a sustained way. Providing credit facilities that bundle access to electricity with appliances can also foster economic activity.

Payment flexibility is particularly important to overcome credit constraints for connection fees in Rwanda (figure 3.6). Twice as many households would rather pay the full price of connection over 24 months than half the price at once. The proportions remain similar even among households in the

Figure 3.6 Willingness to Pay for a Grid Connection in Rwanda

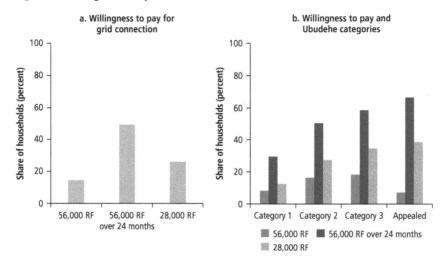

Source: World Bank Multi-Tier Framework data for Rwanda 2017.
Note: Ubudehe is a government program that classifies households according to socioeconomic status.
RF = Rwanda franc.

highest category of Ubudehe, a government program that classifies households according to socioeconomic status.[4]

Housing Quality, Statutory Requirements for Connection, and Prioritization of Needs

The electricity connection to a house requires certain minimum building standards that many existing houses do not meet. Additionally, the qualitative work for this study showed that a significant share of households, especially in rural areas, live in precarious housing and would prioritize housing improvement over electricity services when they have budget constraints.

Reliability Is Central to the Uptake of Grid Electricity

To what extent does the reliability of electricity in the community affect households' decisions to connect to electricity? Supply irregularities in utilities such as electricity affect the connection rate through two main channels.

- First, service disruptions and low voltage reduce the expected benefits of connection, as evidenced by the impact on already-connected households, particularly given that disruptions constrain the ability of these households to exploit electricity for productive uses. This leads prospective households to question their ability to generate enough income to recover their investments in the electricity connection, given the prevailing service quality.

- Second, the possibility of refusing to connect as a form of protest cannot be ignored. Poor service delivery generates distrust among citizens in the ability and willingness of the utility provider to deliver sufficient value for money. Accordingly, unconnected households may resort to illegal connections rather than official connections, thereby stalling official connection rates. Power theft has the potential to exacerbate unreliability—theft affects the revenue performance of the utility and disrupts voltage stability, thereby resulting in localized power outages.[5] In 2015, for instance, Eskom South Africa reported that about US$350 million worth of electricity was lost to theft.[6]

Figure 3.7 shows the relationship between uptake and reliability of grid electricity at the aggregate level. Countries with high uptake of electricity tend to have a higher level of reliability and vice versa. In other words, household connections in communities where access is available tend to be high when supply is reliable. A notable exception is Nigeria, where despite a 100 percent uptake rate,[7] reliability remains a critical obstacle to the electricity sector, given that only 17.5 percent of households have access to reliable electricity.

Figure 3.7 Electricity Uptake and Reliability in Sub-Saharan Africa

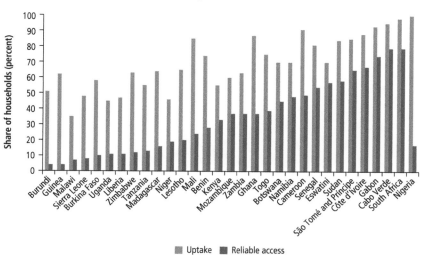

Source: Calculations using data from the Afrobarometer Round VI data set.

At the micro level, there is a strong and positive correlation between household connection rate and the reliability of electricity, as demonstrated in figure 3.8 using data from the Afrobarometer survey and the Global Tracking Framework.

Furthermore, using household data from Kenya, Millien (2017) finds a negative impact of outage intensity on connection rates (see figure 3.9). In other words, an increase in the intensity of power outages in a community reduces the

Figure 3.8 Household Connections and Electricity Reliability in the Community

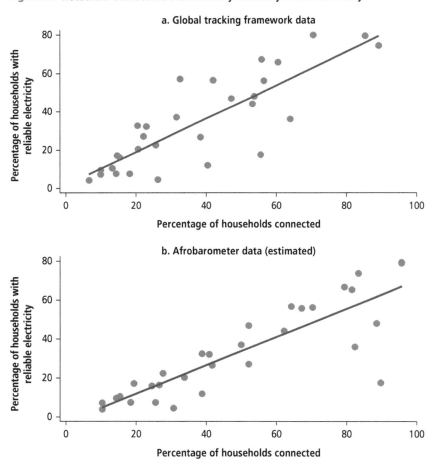

Sources: Calculations using the Afrobarometer and Global Tracking Framework (GTF) data sets. Each data point represents a country.

Figure 3.9 Reliability and the Probability of Connection

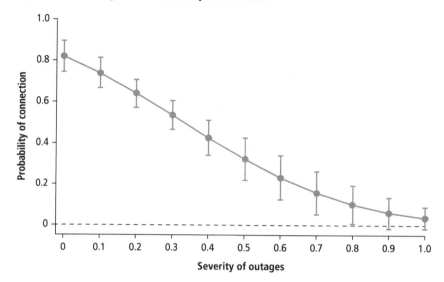

Source: Adapted from Millien 2017.
Note: Figure shows the prediction of connection given the severity of outages.

probability of electricity connection. The unreliable provision of electricity increases the uncertainty associated with the potential net benefits from investments in electrical connection for prospective households.

Improving the Reliability of the Electricity Service Would Encourage Uptake
In Nigeria, 51 percent of connected households reported having electricity only occasionally in the dwelling. This is a key issue because the unreliability of the service affects the value that potential new customers attribute to access. Unreliability has also been reported as a justification for nonpayment of bills. Blackouts are not the only issue customers faced. During brownouts, electricity capacity may be sufficient for lightbulbs but not to power a fan or refrigerator. Service disruptions and low capacity lead to lower benefits of electricity service, which hinders consumers' willingness to connect. Indeed, there is a strong and positive correlation between households' connection rate and the reliability of electricity.

Utilities' Financial Disincentives to Connect Additional Households
For many electricity distributors in Africa, adding a residential customer is unprofitable. The wholesale cost of electricity is high; the regulated retail tariffs are low; and the typical residential user's consumption is low.

The wholesale cost of generating electricity in Africa is high compared with the cost in many other countries. Fossil fuels, especially coal, are the predominant form of generation. In 2015, fossil fuels comprised 74 percent of total generation in the region, with most of the remainder (21 percent) provided by hydroelectricity. Insufficient capacity means that electricity producers often rely on expensive diesel generation to satisfy demand. Inadequate transmission capacity limits the size of the market and restricts the potential for economies of scale in generation. Most electricity in the region is generated and sold by vertically integrated firms, with little transparency on wholesale costs. The wholesale price in the Southern Africa Power Pool market averaged US$76/megawatt hour (MWh) between 2014 and 2016, compared with the average wholesale price of US$35/MWh in the United States in 2015.

In Uganda, in 2011, the median household electricity consumption of grid-connected households was 40 kilowatt hours (kWh) per month. Such low consumption makes it difficult to recover the fixed costs of providing a grid connection using volumetric charges alone. Regulated retail electricity tariffs in many countries have a nonlinear structure, based on increasing block tariffs or volume-differentiated tariffs. In either case, households with low usage pay a low marginal price for an additional unit consumed. For eight countries in Africa, the average price for consuming 50 kWh per month is less than the Southern Africa Power Pool wholesale price. Electricity retailers in these countries would lose money supplying these customers, even before considering the cost of providing the connection.

Conversely, a few countries have very high retail electricity prices (in one case, greater than US$0.50/kWh), likely reflecting the high cost of small-scale diesel generation. Given low consumption, high wholesale prices, and low retail tariffs, adding a residential customer would be unprofitable for most electricity distributors in Africa. Based on these averages, suppose the median new user has electricity consumption of 40 kWh/month, and the wholesale cost of electricity is US$76/MWh. Assume that transmission and distribution losses are 15 percent. Apart from the wholesale cost of electricity, there is assumed to be a fixed annual cost of US$41 per user for administration, billing, and network maintenance. The before-tax retail price in each country is the average shown in figure 3.10.

Distribution utilities are assumed to have an annual discount rate of 5 percent. With these assumptions, the distribution utilities in 15 countries would lose money by adding one more user, before considering any connection costs or charges. Assuming an upfront cost of US$200 to provide a connection, adding consumers would be unprofitable in all but 10 countries (figure 3.11). Distribution utilities in all the remaining countries would need to set a high access charge for it to be profitable to add a user. Under these conditions, high connection charges and low access rates can arise from regulated electricity

Figure 3.10 Average Retail Price Based on Monthly Consumption of 50 kWh

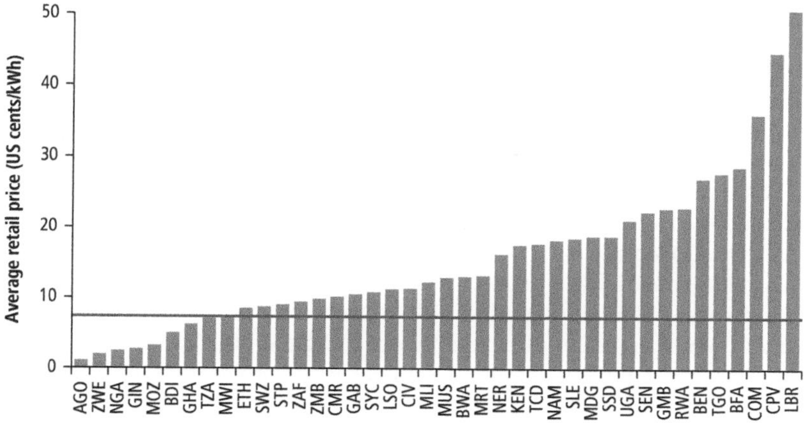

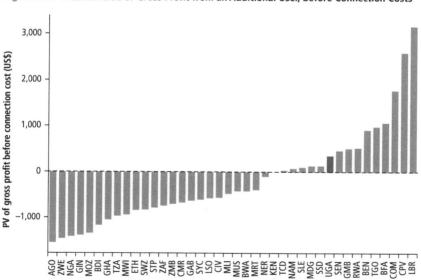

Source: Blimpo, McRae, and Steinbuks 2018.

Figure 3.11 Present Value of Gross Profit from an Additional User, before Connection Costs

Source: Blimpo, McRae, and Steinbuks 2018.
Note: PV = present value.

tariffs that are set too low. The potential losses from connecting additional customers make it optimal for distribution utilities to set high connection charges.
These high charges reduce the demand for connections and recover future
losses from those customers who do connect.

Blimpo, McRae, and Steinbuks (2018) use data from Uganda to estimate a
demand model and analyze the incentives faced by the distribution utility to
seek and connect new customers. The analysis describes the electricity sector
for several countries in Africa and explains the observation of low connection
rates combined with high connection charges. It is closely related to the theoretical literature on optimal two-part tariffs for regulated monopolies. Feldstein
(1972) studies the trade-off between a fixed charge and a marginal price per unit
for a regulated monopoly, assuming all households pay the same prices, in a
setting in which households have different marginal utilities of income. The
value of electrification is the future stream of energy services that the household
receives. It is assumed that an external regulator fixes the marginal price, and
the only choice for the regulated utility is the level of the connection charge.

Connection Charges as a Lever for Utilities to Reduce Losses
Figure 3.12 presents the equilibrium relationship between the rate of electricity
access, connection charges, and regulated tariffs. With a higher regulated electricity price, the optimal connection charge is lower. The estimates indicate that
the maximum profit per actual and potential customer is attained with a

Figure 3.12 Equilibrium Break-Even Connection Charge and Share of Connected Households,
as a Function of the Regulated Price of Electricity

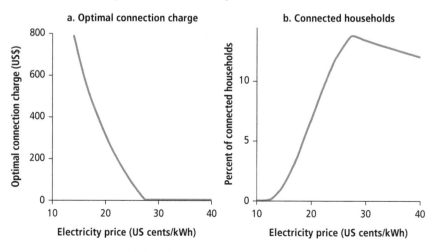

Source: Blimpo, McRae, and Steinbuks 2018.
Note: kWh = kilowatt hours.

connection charge of US$200 to US$300, giving an average gross profit of about US$0.19 per household in the service territory. The profit-maximizing connection charge is higher than the observed connection charges (which vary based on whether new pole installation is required) set by Umeme, Uganda's largest distribution company. Optimal connection charges are lower for higher regulated electricity prices. For an electricity price of US$0.27/kWh, the optimal connection charge would be zero (figure 3.12, panel a), and this connection charge would maximize the number of connected households (figure 3.12, panel b). For electricity prices less than US$0.27/kWh, the connection charge that would maximize utility profits increases, leading to a drop in the number of connected households.

This decline occurs because, in households' connection decisions, the higher upfront connection cost outweighs the value of the lower electricity price. For electricity prices greater than US$0.27/kWh, the number of connected households declines slightly, given that the connection charge remains zero and the value of a connection is lower at higher electricity prices.

Faster Progress Will Require Rising Household Income

Changes in the model's parameters allow for an assessment of the effects of changes in connection charges, the price of kerosene (a substitute), the distance to the distribution network, and increased household income. Figure 3.13 reports the sensitivity analyses. Only in the case in which the regulated tariffs are low and the optimal connection charge is zero does expansion of the network have a significant effect on the number of connected households.

Household income affects the demand for energy, conditional on the choice of fuel, as well as the fuel choice decision directly. Higher household incomes have little effect on the optimal connection charge. However, higher incomes will lead to much higher electricity connection rates for all but the very lowest regulated tariffs.

Accounting for Uptake ahead of Grid Expansion

The discussion in the previous sections cannot be applied to communities that are currently off the grid because they differ in many ways. To provide a sense of uptake in underserved communities, figure 3.14 assesses the overlap between the population in areas on and off the grid, based on a key determinant, that is, income. A perfect overlap suggests that uptake would be similar to that in on-grid areas. The larger the overlap, the more comparable the uptake between the two populations. The first panels in figure 3.14 use only expenditure values, which also serve as a proxy for household income. The second panels add several other factors that determine households' economic status.

The household expenditure profiles are not radically different between the on-grid and off-grid populations in all the countries considered, except for Mauritania. To the extent that income is the key predictor of uptake (using expenditure as a proxy), it would be expected that uptake would remain similar with expansion of the grid. However, when other factors—housing quality (roof, wall, and floor), ownership of assets, and ownership of appliances—are considered, stark differences emerge in most countries (although to a lesser

Figure 3.13 **Sensitivity of Optimal Connection Charges and Share of Connected Households**

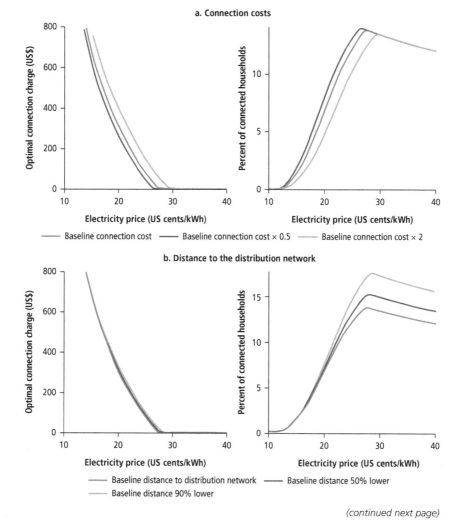

(continued next page)

Figure 3.13 (continued)

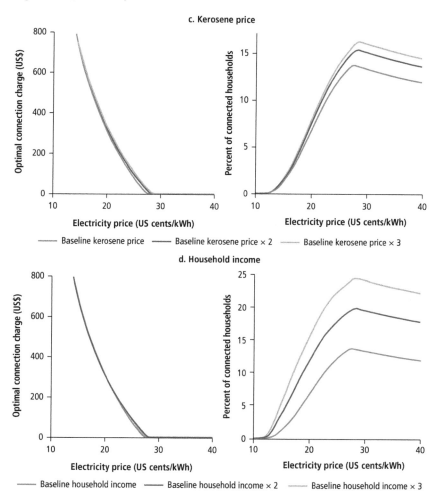

Source: Blimpo, McRae, and Steinbuks 2018.
Note: kWh = kilowatt hours.

extent in Cameroon). It is therefore likely that the uptake gap will increase with grid expansion unless additional measures can be bundled with the expansion. These measures aim to ease the affordability constraints, including household income flows and the connection charges and processes, as well as measures to raise willingness to pay. Enabling the productive use of electricity is a way to address several of these constraints simultaneously.

The analysis of uptake in off-grid areas requires a two-step process consisting of modeling the grid extension first, and then modeling the uptake rate conditioned on grid access. The method used is the Heckman (1976) two-stage estimation procedure to address selection bias, since the grid expansion decision is not random. In this way, the results can be extended to off-grid areas. The findings suggest that the selection of communities for grid expansion does not fully utilize the underlying potential. Strategic targeting could result in greater uptake rates, indicating that the uptake rate in an average rural community is about 8 percent lower than it would be in a randomly selected rural community. Blimpo, Postepska, and Xu (2018). The last two columns in table 3.2 summarize the results of the Heckman selection model

Figure 3.14 Comparison of Communities under a Grid and Those without a Grid

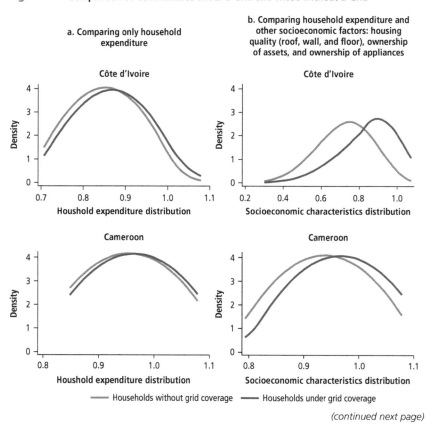

(continued next page)

Figure 3.14 (continued)

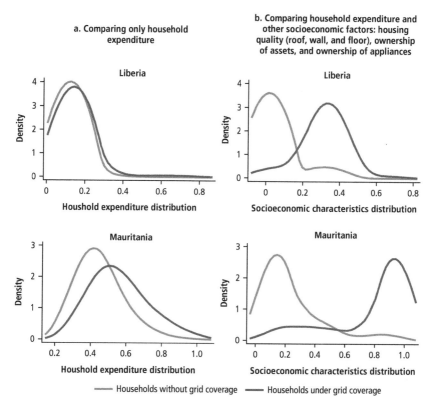

Source: World Bank Living Standards Measurement Study data.
Note: Côte d'Ivoire (2015); Cameroon (2014); Liberia (2014); Mauritania (2014).

for the whole sample and rural areas. The infrastructure and household well-being variables positively affect community-level uptake rates, which is entirely consistent with the findings in the previous section. This provides further evidence that the economic well-being of a community is crucial to achieving a high uptake rate. Hence, economic well-being must precede grid coverage or electricity must enable individuals to increase their economic well-being. Additionally, uptake rates increase when greater shares of households have electricity at least most of the time. Evidence from field work suggests that frequent blackouts experienced in the community can deter unconnected households from connecting.

Table 3.2 Determinants of Uptake: OLS and Heckman Two-Stage Model Results

Variable	OLS All	OLS Rural	Heckman All	Heckman Rural
Population with reliable electricity (%)	0.099***	0.127***	0.100***	0.159***
	(6.426)	(6.384)	(5.508)	(8.843)
Population with a cash-paying job (%)	0.061***	0.059*	0.032***	0.089***
	(3.727)	(2.465)	(1.231)	(3.380)
Households with a high-quality roof (%)	0.185***	0.119***	0.057***	0.041***
	(10.023)	(5.870)	(2.033)	(1.749)
Average wealth index	0.142***	0.209***	0.063***	0.070**
	(3.729)	(3.554)	(0.984)	(1.105)
Control variables	Yes	Yes	Yes	Yes
Mills lambda			−0.326***	−0.155***
			(12.716)	(−5.113)
Number of observations	3,882	1,807	4,328	2,621

Source: Blimpo, Postepska, and Xu 2018.
Note: t statistics are in parentheses. The table reports only significant variables of interest. Control variables include percentage of population employed in the farm sector, percentage of population in clerical occupations, percentage of population with secondary schooling, percentage of population with ethnicity the same as the president, average wealth index, access to water, access to paved roads, access to sewerage, community has a market, community has a school, and community has a bank. OLS = ordinary least squares.
* $p < 0.05$, *** $p < 0.01$, *** $p < 0.001$.

Off-Grid Solutions Can Help Expand Basic Access, but They Face Low Uptake Too

Africa is experiencing an explosion of new technologies, including solar electricity provision. A significant portion of customers currently use solar for lighting, charging mobile phones, and powering a few low-capacity appliances. These relatively basic needs can be met with solar off-grid solutions as an interim step toward higher-tier electricity access. Sales of branded pico (figure 3.15) and home solar systems in Africa have grown sharply (albeit from a low base). Lower prices and mechanisms for quality assurance are needed to achieve significant uptake of these solar solutions. Although such products satisfy current requirements for many, access to higher-tier electrification needs ongoing support to create productive use and generate income and jobs. The manufacture of off-grid components could also be a source of employment through local production of solar-based products.

Quality Assurance Can Help Uptake of Off-Grid Solutions for Basic Access

Over the years, the types of solar products sold in African markets have grown, with varying degrees of reliability and quality. The proliferation of imitation and substandard solar products and their associated suboptimal performance has

Figure 3.15 Annual Sales of Branded Pico Solar Lighting Products in Africa

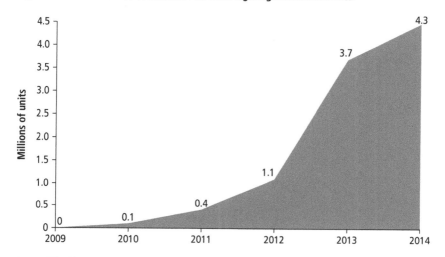

Source: Off-Grid Solar Market Trends Report 2016.
Note: Pico solar or pico pv: compact and lightweight solar photovoltaic panels able to generate a few watts to power a wide range of small and portable devices.

the potential to erode consumer confidence in the solar market (Bloomberg New Energy Finance and Lighting Global 2016). To this end, in 2009, the World Bank Group's Lighting Africa program implemented a quality assurance program that certifies the quality and performance of solar products. This program uses a rigorous testing procedure that has been adopted by the International Electrical Committee.[8] The program has so far yielded significant impacts on the solar lantern market in Africa (and Asia), with the sale of more than 12 million quality-verified products.

Joint research in Senegal by the World Bank and Lighting Africa used a radio campaign to assess the impact of providing information to households on the specifications of the products and how this information affects uptake. The research found that the mass media approach of disseminating information on solar solutions reinforces the adherence of existing customers and moves them up the energy ladder (for example, acquisition of higher-capacity products), but more direct interaction is required to attract new customers (Coville, Orozco, and Reichert 2017).

Another significant result is that among all the attributes, durability seems to matter most in Senegal, with willingness to pay increasing for products with higher expected lifetimes (figure 3.16). One challenge is that no mechanism allows customers to assess durability between low- and high-quality pico photovoltaic products ahead of time.

Figure 3.16 Willingness to Pay and Product Warranty: Evidence from Senegal

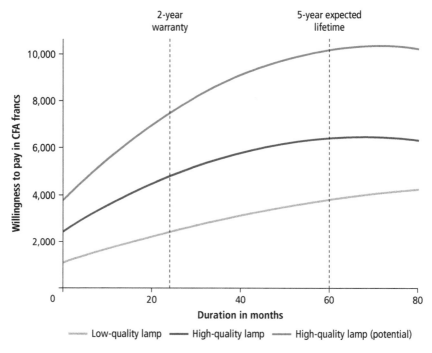

Source: Coville, Orozco, and Reichert 2017.
Note: The functions are plotted based on the estimated intercept, coefficients of expected duration (months), and its square. The square of duration is insignificant for Low-quality lamp. Vertical lines indicate the mean perceived duration, warranty period, and expected lifespan of a high-quality lamp.

Reliability and Service Quality Matter for Willingness to Pay for Off-Grid Solutions

The impact of service quality is also associated with off-grid electricity. The product quality and capacity of off-grid solutions are key determinants of uptake because they determine the benefits of these energy sources for the households that adopt them.

Peters and Sievert (2015) provide evidence of a high preference among households without electricity in Senegal, Burkina Faso, and Rwanda, for electricity with sufficient capacity to support the use of appliances such as televisions and refrigerators relative to services that only support appliances such as radios, lighting, and mobile phone charging. This preference is reflected in high (stated) willingness to pay for high-capacity electricity services, as shown in figure 3.17.

Figure 3.17 **Willingness to Pay for Different Service Levels (monthly fees)**

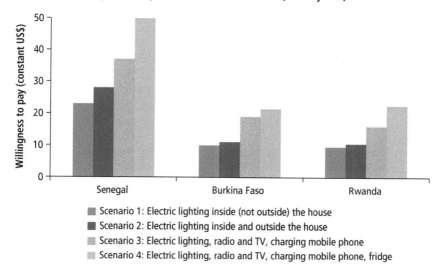

Source: Adapted from Peters and Sievert 2015.

Electricity for What? Productive Use, Income Generation, and Jobs at Center Stage

Using electricity to generate economic activity and increase productivity is essential to justifying the required high investment. Productive use is also critical for creating higher consumption to make utilities more sustainable. Productive use refers to income-generating activities that depend on electricity as an input, such as manufacturing and other industrial activities. The services sector also needs electricity for lighting, refrigeration, air conditioning, and powering computer and office equipment.

The productive use of rural electrification is particularly relevant for Africa, given that the majority of the population resides in rural areas. Examples of productive electricity use in rural settings include the following:

> In rural contexts in developing countries, typical productive uses can be found in agro-processing (for example, grain milling), various manufacturing industries such as carpentry, tailoring, welding and looming, and in the service sector, e.g., in bars and restaurants that use electricity for lighting, sound systems and refrigeration, as well as for charging mobile phones. (Brüderle, Attigah, and Bodenbender 2011, 12)

The provision of electricity may be insufficient by itself to generate productive uses unless it is accompanied by parallel support measures such as raising aware-ness, providing access to finance for newly electrified small businesses, and investing in other infrastructure, especially roads (Brüderle, Attigah, and Bodenbender 2011). Some evidence also suggests that the provision of off-grid electricity in rural areas may not have the economic impact of grid electricity. Business creation in Namibian households with grid electricity was found to be fourfold greater than in households with off-grid solar systems (World Bank 2005). One reason is the low power output of basic solar systems, which is insuf-ficient to operate appliances such as refrigerators and washing machines (figure 3.18). Home solar is not a substitute for grid energy for major appliance use. Environmental advantages will be limited in countries where grid power is mainly generated from non–fossil fuel sources (Lee, Miguel, and Wolfram 2016). Although prices have dropped, powerful solar kits are not affordable for many rural dwellers. Low-power, off-grid solutions can serve as interim solutions for the poor until higher-tier access becomes more affordable over time.

Given the large and youthful population in most African countries, creating jobs is a top priority. People identify unemployment as the most pressing challenge on which governments should focus (figure 3.19). Without electricity contributing to job creation and rising incomes, the vast majority of the population cannot

Figure 3.18 Sustainable Energy for All Electricity Access Tiers

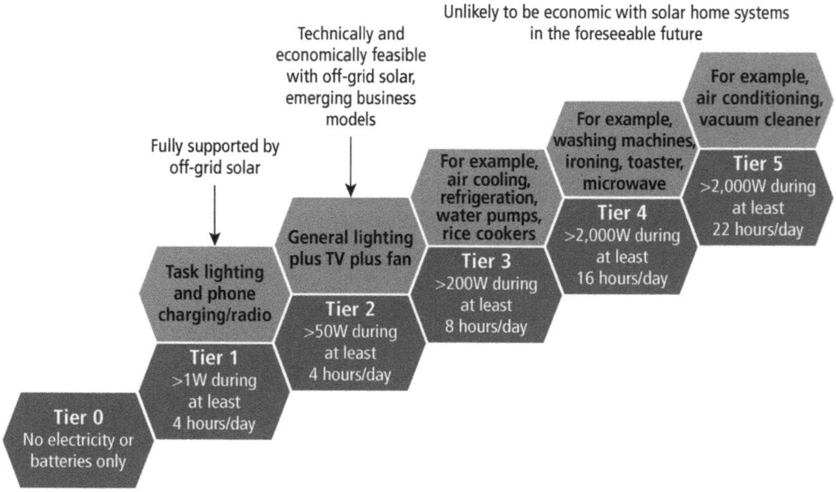

Source: Bloomberg New Energy Finance and Lighting Global 2016.
Note: Sustainable Energy for All calls for tiers 2 to 5 to be affordable and for tiers 3 to 5 to be reliable and legal.
W = watts.

Figure 3.19 Most Important Problems in Sub-Saharan Africa

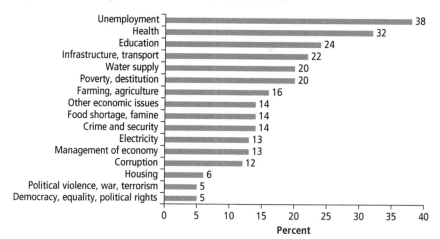

Source: Calculations using Afrobarometer Round VI data 2014/15.
Note: The question is formulated as follows: "In your opinion, what are the most important problems facing this country that government should address?" The respondents could give up to three responses. The figure shows the percentage of respondents naming the problem as one of their three responses.

afford meaningful usage with their current level of income. Linking electrification rollout to job creation is an excellent way to attract investment, since higher incomes are likely to increase electricity uptake and consumption and contribute to financial viability in the sector. As an example, South Africa's grid rollout to poor rural and predominantly black citizens generated higher uptake among households operating micro, small, and medium-sized enterprises. Prasad and Dieden (2007) estimate that there may have been an increase of 40–53 percent in the activities of such enterprises attributable to the electric grid rollout in South Africa.

Conclusion

The share of households located in areas off the electrical grid is still large, and efforts to bring electricity to these areas should be part of any development strategy. However, those efforts should be accompanied by policy measures to spur uptake and consumption in areas already covered by the grid as well those off the grid. People's inability to purchase desired appliances is a deterrent to access to electricity. High electricity connection charges are a primary barrier to electricity access and a significant contributor to low electrification rates in Africa. Additional constraints include irregular household income flows, which limit the ability to pay regular bills, and poor housing quality. Although appropriate measures to address these issues will help in the short run, a more fundamental question is the reason utilities set high connection charges in the first place. The household and utility model demonstrates how low regulated tariffs and the overall low level of consumption of an average household lead to high connection charges and low electrification rates. Real and financially sustainable progress will come only with rising household incomes. Electrification can play a crucial role in creating opportunities for income-generating activities. For that to happen, electricity provision must come with the necessary capacity and be reliable, and electrification efforts should be accompanied by the provision of complementary factors. Chapters 4 and 5 address these issues in more depth.

Notes

1. Uptake is defined as the number of households that have access to electricity divided by the number of households under the grid.
2. The Energy Sector Management Assistance Program defines household affordability as no more than 5 percent of total income dedicated to paying for energy needs (Kojima and Trimble 2016).
3. Republic of Rwanda, Rural Electrification Strategy, 2016.
4. These socioeconomic factors include possession of housing, earnings, and food security.
5. For instance, electricity thieves may unknowingly feed power back into the electricity lines, thereby causing a blowout of the system (https://www.safeelectricity.org /information-center/library-of-articles/57-meter-tampering/124-paying-the-price -of-power-theft, accessed December 2017).
6. Exchange rate of 1 South African rand to US$0.074.
7. The uptake rate refers to the share of households connected in a community with access.
8. https://www.iecee.org/dyn/www/f?p=106:49:0::::FSP_STD_ID:20378.

References

Bacon, R., S. Bhattacharya, and M. Kojima. 2010. *Expenditure of Low-Income Households on Energy: Evidence from Africa and Asia.* Washington, DC: World Bank. https://openknowledge.worldbank.org/handle/10986/16297.

Blimpo, M. P., K. Gbenyo, C. Meniago, and J. T. Mensah. 2018. "Stylized Facts on the Cost of Household Connection to the Electricity Grid in African Countries." Working Paper, World Bank, Washington, DC.

Blimpo, M. P., S. McRae, and J. Steinbuks. 2018. "Why Are Connection Charges So High?: An Analysis of the Electricity Sector in Sub-Saharan Africa." Policy Research Working Paper No. 8407. World Bank, Washington, DC.

Blimpo, M. P., A. Postepska, and Y. Xu. 2018. "Why Is Household Electricity Uptake Low in Sub-Saharan Africa?" Working Paper, World Bank, Washington, DC.

Bloomberg New Energy Finance and Lighting Global. 2016. *Off-Grid Solar Market Trends Report*. Washington, DC: World Bank. https://www.esmap.org/node/71032.

Brüderle, A., B. Attigah, and M. Bodenbender. 2011. *Productive Use of Energy: PRODUSE: A Manual for Electrification Practitioners*. Eschborn, Germany: European Union Energy Initiative-Partnership Dialogue Facility. http://www.euei-pdf.org/sites/default/files/field_publication_file/150907_euei_productive-use-manual_rz_04_web.pdf.

Coville, A., V. Orozco, and A. Reichert. 2017. "Paying Attention to Technology Innovations—Experimental Evidence from Solar Lighting in Africa." Unpublished, World Bank, Washington, DC.

Enerdata. 2015. EnerMonthly. Retrieved from Enerdata database.

Feldstein, M. 1972. "Equity and Efficiency in Public Sector Pricing: The Optimal Two-Part Tariff." *Quarterly Journal of Economics* 86 (2): 175–87.

Golumbeanu, R., and D. Barnes. 2013. "Connection Charges and Electricity Access in Sub-Saharan Africa." Policy Research Working Paper 6511, World Bank, Washington, DC.

Heckman, J. 1976. "The Common Structure of Statistical Models of Truncation, Sample Selection and Limited Dependent Variables and a Simple Estimator for Such Models." *Annals of Economic and Social Measurement* 5 (4): 475–92.

Kojima, M., and C. Trimble. 2016. *Making Power Affordable for Africa and Viable for Its Utilities*. Washington, DC: World Bank. http://documents.worldbank.org/curated/en/293531475067040608/Making-power-affordable-for-Africa-and-viable-for-its-utilities.

Lall, S. V., J. V. Henderson, and A. J. Venables. 2017. *Africa's Cities: Opening Doors to the World*. Washington, DC: World Bank.

Lee, K., E. Miguel, and C. Wolfram. 2016. "Appliance Ownership and Aspirations among Electric Grid and Home Solar Households in Rural Kenya." Working Paper 21949, National Bureau of Economic Research, Cambridge, MA. http://www.nber.org/papers/w21949 or doi:10.3386/w21949.

Millien, A. 2017. "Electricity Supply Reliability and Households Decision to Connect to the Grid." Working Paper P192, Fondation pour les études et recherches sur le développement international. https://econpapers.repec.org/paper/fdiwpaper/3868.htm.

Peters, J., and M. Sievert. 2015. "On-Grid and Off-Grid Rural Electrification—Impacts and Cost Considerations Revisited." *Revue d'économie du développement* 23: 85–104.

Prasad, G., and S. Dieden. 2007. "Does Access to Electricity Enable the Uptake of Small and Medium Enterprises in South Africa?" Paper presented at the Domestic Use of Energy Conference, Cape Town, South Africa. http://citeseerx.ist.psu.edu/viewdoc/download?doi=10.1.1.492.8722&rep=rep1&type=pdf.

Thaler, B. R. 1980. "Toward a Positive Theory of Consumer Choice." *Journal of Economic Behavior and Organization* 1 (1): 39–60.

von Neumann, J., and O. Morgenstern. 1944. *Theory of Games and Economic Behavior*. Princeton, NJ: Princeton University Press.

World Bank. 2005. *Power Sector Reform in Africa: Assessing Impact on Poor People*. Washington, DC: World Bank.

———. 2018. *Doing Business 2018: Reforming to Create Jobs*. Washington, DC: World Bank.

Chapter 4

Prioritizing Reliability for Economic Impact

Chapter 1 highlights the pervasiveness of unreliable electricity in Sub-Saharan African (hereafter African or SSA) countries. If electricity is to contribute to income generation and to job creation, reliability needs to receive more attention. Furthermore, uptake is adversely affected if those who are under the grid but not connected put value on the reliability of the services, as shown in chapter 3. Likewise, unreliability not only affects existing firms; it also inhibits the entry of new firms in sectors that require electricity. Addressing reliability is one of the ways to simultaneously address the economic development imperative and improve the financial viability of electricity service providers. See box 4.1 for a definition of reliability.

Unreliability Affects Economic Activities through Several Channels

The provision of reliable electricity affects economic transformation through at least three pathways: lowering the cost of doing business, thereby increasing business entry; increasing the performance of existing firms through higher productivity and revenue; and increasing the welfare and quality of life of households, thereby enhancing the offer of productive labor services.

First, the provision of reliable electricity reduces the cost of doing business. New firms are established, while existing businesses that would otherwise have shut down in the presence of unreliable electricity provision are sustained. Second, productivity and revenue gains are associated with reliable electricity provision, thereby boosting the performance of the industrial sector. Third, access to reliable electricity improves the welfare and quality of life of households so that they can offer productive labor services to the industrial sector.

BOX 4.1

Defining Reliability

Reliability is used broadly to refer to access to electricity that is stable, without fluctuations in voltage, always available, and capable of supporting appliance usage subject to the voltage capacity of the grid line. The two main risks to reliability are outages (blackouts) and brownouts. *Outages* refer to the total loss of electric power in each location and period. Outages vary from short to long term. *Brownouts* refer to a drop in the voltage of an electric system. Whereas outages involve a complete loss of electric power, brownouts entail a partial loss of power. Brownouts constrain the use of high-voltage appliances (such as refrigerators, televisions, and air conditioners) and often result in malfunction of electric appliances.

These risks to reliability have implications for the definition of access to electricity. For example, although a household or business may be connected, the service flow may not be enough to support its productive needs. These concerns have led to the development of an alternate measure of access, referred to as the Multi-Tier Framework (MTF). The MTF provides a multidimensional measure of access that incorporates capacity, duration, quality, reliability, legality, and safety. This measure accounts not only for the risks to service provision, but also appliance usage. The MTF presents an ordinal measure ranging from tier 0 to tier 5, where tier 0 refers to no access, and tier 5 represents the highest level of electricity availability and utilization, as shown in figure 4A.1 in annex 4A. The advantage of the MTF measure is that it offers more information about access, thereby allowing for differentiation of service levels. The tier classification suggests that for full utilization of electricity for productive socioeconomic impacts, end users (households and firms) would require access to a minimum of tier 4. The remainder of the chapter uses data on outages, brownouts, and the MTF access tiers to demonstrate the role of access to reliable electricity for economic transformation.

For example, the reliable provision of electricity exerts positive impacts on the delivery of social services, such as health care, education, and entertainment—all of which influence the quality of life. These pathways work through the impact of reliability on commercial use (industry), households, and the provision of social services, as shown in figure 4.1.

Unreliability Creates Uncertainty in the Business Climate

Irregularities in the supply of electricity lead to high production costs in the commercial sector. They also create uncertainties in the business climate, especially given that electricity is an integral input for modern firms. The World Bank's *Doing Business Report*, for instance, cites electricity outages as a major constraint in the business sector of most African economies, serving as a major component of the cost of doing business in the region. Therefore, lack of

Figure 4.1 **Effects of Electricity Reliability on Economic Transformation**

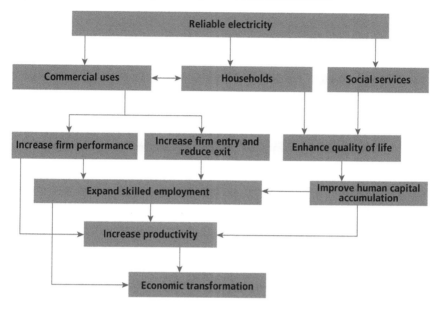

reliability negatively affects the incentives of potential entrepreneurs to establish businesses and reduces the business density in the region. This is even more critical for Africa in this era where digital technologies are offering many opportunities for countries to build up a strong digital economy (box 4.2).

The prevalence of electricity outages and the associated cost to firms also has implications for the survival of existing firms. Economic theory suggests that for any profit-maximizing firm, high production losses or costs resulting from the impact of outages can push firms to relocate to areas with reliable access to electricity (under the assumption of perfect mobility of labor and capital) or shut down production to avoid investment losses. Fisher-Vanden, Mansur, and Wang (2015) show that Chinese manufacturing firms respond to electricity outages by outsourcing production to firms in regions where the supply of electricity is reliable.

Persistent outages can constrain expansion in the industrial and services sectors, thereby reducing labor demand and employment. The provision of reliable electricity has the potential to increase the growth of the industrial sector by increasing business entry and the survival of existing firms. This will eventually create employment for skilled labor, increase productivity, and, in the long run, boost the pace of economic transformation. Box 4.3 presents suggestive evidence of the effect of electricity outages on business entry.

BOX 4.2

Reliable Electricity and the Digital Economy

Many countries in Africa seek to diversify their economies with information and communication technologies (ICT), including expanding ICT as a sector in its own right and increasing its use in enterprises. One of the core ICT infrastructure elements is the data center. These facilities are a vital engine of the digital economy, storing data, hosting websites, and enabling cloud-based applications. Data centers are virtual data factories that make productive use of electricity with measurable economic impacts on gross domestic product, employment, and government tax revenue (Dutch Datacenter Association 2017).

Data centers consume considerable electricity in powering computer equipment and keeping it cool. In 2011, Google reported that it used 260 megawatts of electric power for its data centers (Glanz 2011), which is more than the 2014 installed capacity in 19 African countries (Trimble et al. 2016). Data centers require high levels of reliability to ensure the seamless, nonstop flow of data. Reliability is defined by industry standards as ranging from 99.67 percent availability with no more than 29 hours of interruption per year for tier 1 data centers, to 99.995 percent reliability with just 0.8 hour of interruption per year for the highest tier 4 centers. Most African nations would find it difficult to meet even tier 1 reliability. The standards also call for a guaranteed source of electrical backup that can power the center for at least half a day (Uptime Institute 2012).

Enterprise-grade reliability requirements for industry certification generally rule out the feasibility of large data centers in many African countries. Because of the region's challenging environment for reliable and inexpensive electricity, most businesses host their data outside the region. This results in a large volume of data transmitted to overseas data centers, requiring significant amounts of international Internet bandwidth. The cost of the bandwidth combined with overseas hosting prices triggers payments from Africa to overseas companies of several hundred million U.S. dollars per year, negatively affecting the region's balance of payments. It also takes longer to access overseas data centers, which increases latency. Security is an issue because increasing amounts of government, business, and personal information are transmitted abroad with vague data protection.

Despite concerns about reliability, the idea of installing large data centers in the region to achieve better latency and reduce the cost of international bandwidth is receiving growing interest. In 2017, Microsoft, one of the world's largest owners of data centers, announced it would build two data centers in South Africa to support its cloud-based services. Notably, South Africa's electricity supply is considered the second most reliable in the region after Mauritius (Oyuke, Halley Penar, and Howard 2016). The new data centers will be faster compared with accessing cloud services in Europe or the United States; international connectivity costs will be reduced; and trust will be increased, given that the centers will have to comply with South Africa's data protection law (Marston 2017). Electricity reliability is critical for other countries in the region that want to develop their digital economies.

BOX 4.3

Electricity Outages, Entrepreneurship, and Business Entry

Empirical evidence on the effects of electricity outages on firm entry and exit is relatively scant. The study by Mensah (2018) presents evidence on the extent to which persistent outages affect firms' entry into the industrial sector. The first piece of evidence is the cross-country correlation between the level of self-reported outages by firms and business entry density (the number of newly registered businesses per 1,000 people), as shown in figure B4.3.1, panel a. The figure shows that higher outage

Figure B4.3.1 Effects of Electricity Outages on Entrepreneurship and Firm Entry

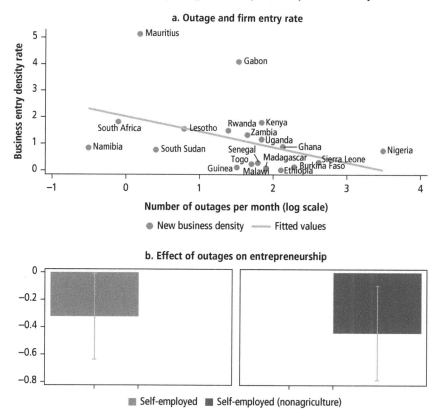

Source: Estimates from Enterprise Survey 2006–16 and Afrobarometer survey 2014/15.
Note: Panel b reports coefficients of outages in a community in an instrumental variable regression. The two dependent variables are whether the individual is self-employed and self-employed in the nonagriculture sector. The regressions include individual, community, and country controls. The confidence intervals are represented by vertical lines.

(continued next page)

BOX 4.3 (continued)

intensity is negatively associated with business entry density in Africa. In other words, firm entry tends to be higher in countries with more reliable access to electricity. Although this result is a mere correlation, it is indicative of the potential effect of unreliability in electricity supply on the expansion of the industrial sector.

To buttress the argument, panel b of figure B4.3.1 presents econometric estimates of the effects of outages on entrepreneurship, using household data from the 2014/15 round of the Afrobarometer survey (Mensah 2018). The estimates were obtained from an instrumental variable regression, thus enabling causal interpretation (Mensah 2018). The results suggest that outages reduce the probability of individuals establishing a business (self-employment) by about 32 percent. The impact is even higher for business establishments in the nonfarm sector, approximately 44 percent.

Unreliability Constrains the Performance of Existing Firms

Over the past century, electricity has become an essential input for the industrial and services sectors. Unreliable provision of electricity, as evidenced by persistent outages, exerts a significant impact on firms because it constrains their production and service delivery. Electricity outages affect existing firms in myriad ways, including but not limited to input choices, investment, revenue, and productivity (Allcott, Collard-Wexler, and O'Connell 2016). Empirical evidence on the effects of electricity outages suggests significant revenue and productivity losses too (Allcott, Collard-Wexler, and O'Connell 2016; Mensah 2017). Although some firms attempt to mitigate the negative impact of electricity outages on their activities through electricity self-generation (for example, generators and minithermal plants), these coping strategies are associated with high costs, thereby affecting competitiveness (Alby, Dethier, and Straub 2013; Steinbuks and Foster 2010). For example, Steinbuks and Foster (2010) show that African firms incur high costs in electricity self-generation because of high fuel cost, which is nearly three times the cost of grid electricity. Similarly, a recent study finds differential effects of more than 30 percentage points of outages on firm revenues between firms that use generators and those that do not (Cole et al. 2018). Alternatively, firms respond to electricity outages by substituting away from electricity-intensive production to less electricity-intensive production (Fisher-Vanden, Mansur, and Wang 2015). Voltage fluctuations (brownouts) are another aspect of reliability. One study finds that one-third of enterprises in western Tanzania suffered appliance damage from voltage fluctuations (Bensch et al. 2017).

Thus, electricity outages negatively affect the performance of firms through their impacts on input use and allocation and production cost. The associated productivity losses may result in job losses (unemployment) and slow the pace of growth in the industrial and services sectors. These effects suggest that the provision of reliable electricity can enhance the pace of industrial development through a transition from low-tech production to high-tech, energy-intensive production.

Household Welfare and Quality of Life Are also Affected

Electricity improves the welfare of households because it enables the use of appliances such as televisions, washing machines, lightbulbs, radios, and rechargeable devices like cell phones and personal computers. Unreliable access to electricity negatively affects the welfare of households. Frequent outages limit households' ability to engage in productive, educational, and recreational activities during nighttime. With a regular supply of electricity, households can engage in productive activities, such as operating a home business beyond daytime, thereby increasing income. With regular electricity supply, children can study at night, thereby improving their educational outcomes (Adamba 2018; Dasso, Fernandez, and Ñopo 2015; Lipscomb, Mobarak, and Barham 2013).

Chakravorty, Pelli, and Marchand (2014) evaluate the impact of electrification on Indian households by comparing the impact of connecting households with the impact of the quality of supply that households receive. The study uses household panel data from 1994 to 2005 and the spatial and time variations in the rollout of electricity transmission lines as an instrument to identify causally the impact of access and quality of supply on households' nonagricultural income. The results suggest that although the impact of electricity connection on household income is quantitatively strong and positive, the impact is even stronger (quantitatively) when the quality of supply is considered. Specifically, Chakravorty, Pelli, and Marchand (2014) find that access to electricity increases household incomes by 9 percent. In other words, being connected to electricity has a positive impact on household income. However, the effect is larger (28.6 percent) for households with reliable access to electricity. Samad and Zhang (2016) analyze the socioeconomic impact of household access to reliable electricity in India. They conclude that the impact of electrification is underestimated if reliability is not taken into account (see figure 4.2).

These findings underscore the importance of reliability in realizing the potential benefits of electricity.

Outages generate a "demographic footprint" (Burlando 2014a, 2014b; Fetzer, Pardo, and Shanghavi 2018). Outages constrain households' participation in social activities and other recreational activities, especially at night, resulting in unintended spillovers on fertility rates. Using data from

Figure 4.2 Socioeconomic Impact of Reliable Electricity in India

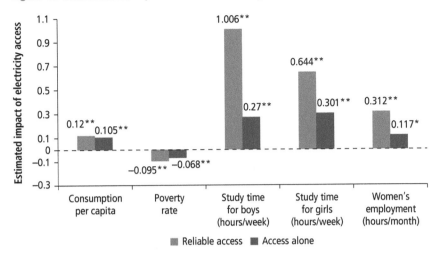

Source: Adapted from Samad and Zhang 2016.
Note: The estimates were obtained from a propensity-score-weighted fixed-effects model.
** $p < 0.05$; * $p < 0.1$.

a unique natural experiment on an unanticipated power crisis in Zanzibar, Tanzania, in 2008, Burlando (2014a, 2014b) provides evidence of a strong externality effect of the power crisis on fertility and child health. Burlando (2014a) shows that the one-month-long power crisis in Zanzibar led to a baby boom 8 to 10 months after the crisis. Burlando (2014b) finds that children who were exposed to the crisis in utero had, on average, lower birth weights—an impact driven by the negative income shock associated with the crisis. Thus, outages impose a nontrivial impact on the welfare of households, which eventually can negatively affect the productivity of labor supplied by households.

Furthermore, the provision of reliable electricity affects the quality of social services, such as hospitals, schools, street lighting, and entertainment. For example, outages constrain the provision of efficient health care in hospitals and clinics, especially at night, since lighting plays a critical role in health care delivery. These services are important for the quality of life, with direct and indirect impacts on human capital accumulation.

To accelerate the pace of economic transformation, countries must not only focus on expanding access to electricity; they must also pay careful attention to the quality of electricity supplied, because end users will foster the productive uses of electricity for development. Even slower progress, but with reliable access, may be a better option than universal access with pervasive unreliability, which may defeat the purpose of electrification.

Reliability and Economic Impact: Recent Evidence from Africa

Although access to electricity is important, reliability matters even more if the impact of electrification is to be fully harnessed. This section examines the effect of reliability on economic activities.

The impact of reliability is multifaceted because it affects all stakeholders in the electricity sector: end users, utility companies, and governments. An unreliable supply of electricity affects end users—households and industry (firms)—negatively by constraining their utilization of electricity for productive and nonproductive uses (Allcott, Collard-Wexler, and O'Connell 2016; Chakravorty, Pelli, and Marchand 2014). From the perspective of the utility, unreliability is a symptom of operational and technical inefficiencies and thus affects the utility's revenue and productivity performance. Persistent outages and poor provision of electricity undoubtedly have negative political economy implications because they affect the general performance of the economy, with potential spillover effects on election cycles (Andersen and Dalgaard 2013; Baskaran, Min, and Uppal 2015). The following subsections document the impact of electricity outages on firms, households, and government.

Power Outages Are a Major Drag on Firm Productivity and Competitiveness in Africa

Electricity is a key input in production, yet firms in many developing countries struggle to gain access to reliable and uninterrupted provision of electricity (Alby, Dethier, and Straub 2013; Allcott, Collard-Wexler, and O'Connell 2016; Eifert, Gelb, and Ramachandran 2008; Mensah 2016).

Mensah (2018) estimates the causal effect of electricity outages on the output and productivity of firms in 23 countries in Africa, using data from World Bank Enterprise Surveys between 2006 and 2016. Box 4.4 presents a brief overview of the countries, data, and method used in the estimation. The results of the estimation (in figure 4.3) show a strong negative effect of outages on the value-added output and productivity of firms in the region: for every percentage point increase in the frequency of electricity outages experienced by firms, real value added (output) declines by 3.3 percent. Similarly, the effect on firms' revenue is nontrivial, given that a percentage point increase in outage frequency results in a 2.7 percent loss in firm revenue. To what extent do these losses in output and revenue translate into productivity losses?

BOX 4.4

Study Location, Data, and Methodology for Analysis of the Impact of Outages on Firm Performance

To estimate the effects of electricity outages on firms' performance, the analysis relies on firm-level data from Angola, Benin, Botswana, Burkina Faso, Cameroon, the Democratic Republic of Congo, Côte d'Ivoire, Eswatini, Ethiopia, The Gambia, Ghana, Guinea, Madagascar, Mozambique, Namibia, Nigeria, Rwanda, Senegal, South Sudan, Sudan, Tanzania, Togo, and Zambia. The countries were surveyed between 2006 and 2016 (map B4.4.1). For causal identification of the impacts of outages, the firm-level data are combined with georeferenced data on the electricity transmission network in Africa to create an index of technical losses in electricity transmission, which was used as an instrument for electricity outages. The estimations were performed in an instrumental variable regression framework. Details of the estimation equation and procedure are presented in annex 4A.

Map B4.4.1 Countries Included in the Analysis of the Impacts of Electricity Outages on Firms

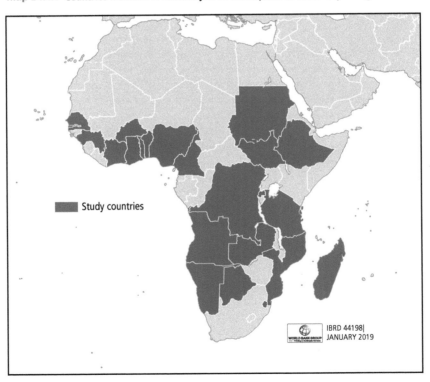

Source: Enterprise Surveys.

Figure 4.3 Effect of Electricity Outages on Output, Revenue, and Productivity

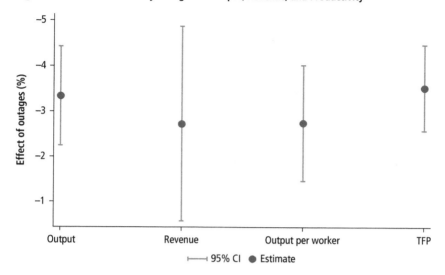

Source: Adapted from Mensah 2018.
Note: CI = confidence interval; TFP = total factor productivity.

To answer this question, the analysis estimates the impact of outages on two measures of productivity: value added per worker and total factor productivity. The results suggest that outages account for a 2.7 percent loss in value added per worker and a 3.5 percent loss in total factor productivity of firms in the study countries.

These results highlight the importance of reliable electricity provision for the performance of the industrial and services sectors.

In addition to the direct impacts of electricity outages on firm performance, there are indirect effects associated with outages. Persistent electricity outages may affect the competitiveness of firms, particularly in exports. To be competitive in international markets, firms, especially those engaged in processing, require reliable electricity to run production lines efficiently because reliance on self-generated electricity, with its attendant costs, increases the cost of production, thereby translating into high output prices. This requirement affects the competitiveness of firms, particularly in external markets, given that they compete with firms from economies with plausibly reliable access to electricity. As shown by Verhoogen (2008) and Melitz (2003), within each industry, the most productive firms can enter export markets; such firms, in turn, affect the labor market through wages and labor demand. Any negative shock to productivity (such as outages) is likely to affect the export competitiveness of firms

Figure 4.4 Electricity Outages, Trade Competitiveness, and Labor Demand

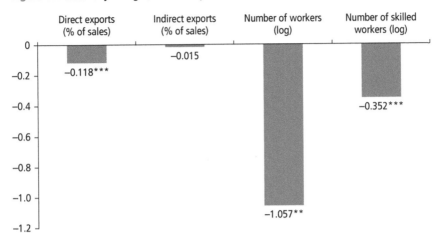

Source: Estimates using Enterprise Survey 2006–16.
Note: The reported coefficients are for ln(Outages) obtained from an estimation equation using the instrumental variable regression approach.
*** $p < 0.01$; ** $p < 0.05$.

in the industry and the ability of firms to venture into export markets. Figure 4.4 shows the effects of outages on the export competitiveness of firms. The results again reveal a negative impact of outages on direct exports: a 1 percentage point increase in outage frequency results in a 0.12 percent reduction in the share of sales from direct exports.[1] However, there is no statistically significant effect on indirect exports.

Given the negative impact of outages on the productivity and trade competitiveness of firms, it is likely that firms will respond to these impacts by altering their input demand. Firms may respond flexibly by changing their production schedules, such that they shut down during outage periods and resume work when power is available (Abeberese, Ackah, and Asuming 2017). In other instances, especially during an intense power crisis, firms may respond by laying off workers to mitigate the rising cost of production. Figure 4.4 shows evidence that firms in Africa respond to these outages by reducing labor demand. Specifically, a percentage point increase in outages results in approximately 1.1 percent and 0.35 percent reductions in the number of workers and skilled workers, respectively, employed by firms in the region.

To understand the impact of electricity outages on firm performance and the associated coping strategies, box 4.5 presents evidence from a case study of the power crisis in Ghana.

Effects of a Power Crisis on Small Firms in Ghana

Over the past three decades, Ghana has experienced several power crisis episodes, largely linked to rainfall variability and the country's overreliance on its main hydro-dam on the Volta River. The most recent and perhaps longest episode occurred between 2012 and 2015. The crisis led to an electricity rationing program. During the peak of the crisis, electricity end users were guaranteed between 12 and 13 hours of supply within every 36-hour period (Abeberese, Ackah, and Asuming 2017).[a] In some instances, however, the number of hours of electricity received by end users was even less than the stipulated duration because of other unforeseen disruptions to the network (Abeberese, Ackah, and Asuming 2017). The implications of this crisis on the performance of the economy were severe.

Using survey data on small and medium-sized manufacturing firms in Ghana, Abeberese, Ackah, and Asuming (2017) estimate the effect of the energy crisis on the productivity and employment of these firms, as well as their coping strategies to mitigate the effects of the crisis. The study estimates firms' willingness to pay (WTP) to avert future outages. The findings from the study reveal that the power crisis led to a 10 percent reduction in the monthly productivity of small and medium-sized manufacturing firms in the country. However, there was no effect on labor demand by these firms resulting in employee layoffs. The authors find that firms adopted a mix of strategies aimed at mitigating the impact of the crisis on their activities, including reducing operating hours, relying on electricity self-generation (generators), changing production time, and switching to the production of less electricity-intensive (reliant) products and processes, as shown in figure B4.5.1.

Figure B4.5.1 Coping Strategies of Firms in Ghana

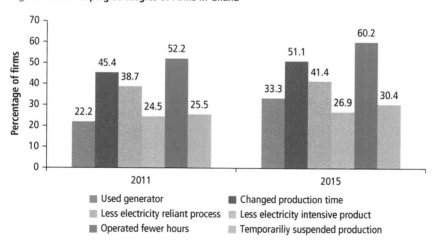

Source: Adapted from Abeberese, Ackah, and Assuming 2017.

(continued next page)

BOX 4.5 (continued)

Another relevant finding of the study is firms' WTP to avert future outages, as shown in figure B4.5.2. Overall, the average firm is willing to pay an extra 12.6 percent of its monthly electricity bill to avert future outages. Interestingly, these WTP estimates are less than the additional cost incurred for electricity self-generation by these firms.

Figure B4.5.2 Willingness to Pay and Electricity Expenditure of Firms in Ghana

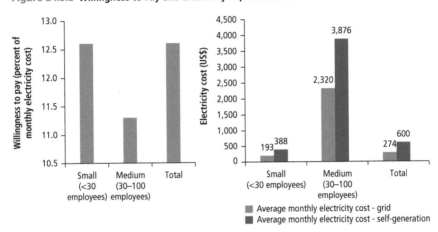

a. Hardy and McCasland (2017) also examine the effects of the Ghanaian Dumsor energy crisis of 2014–15 on small firms in Ghana. They find that each additional blackout day is associated with an 11 percent decrease in firms' weekly profits, on average.

Power Outages and Households' Welfare: Evidence from Africa

Evidence from Mensah (2018) reveals a substantial negative impact of outages on employment (figure 4.5). Outages in a community reduce the probability of employment by approximately 35 percentage points. The impact is even higher (55 percentage points) if only employment in the nonfarm sector is considered.

This evidence gives credence to the theory that the persistence of electricity outages can constrain efforts toward economic transformation by reducing skilled-sector employment. The analysis finds that electricity outages in a community reduce the probability of skilled employment by about 27 percent. These results again underscore the economic importance of not just access to electricity, but more importantly, reliable access. Figure 4.5 illustrates how reliable electricity is crucial for African countries to develop their economies. Additional evidence from the latest Multi-Tier Framework surveys on the relationship between quality of electricity provision and employment is provided in box 4.6.

Figure 4.5 Effects of Electricity Outages on Employment

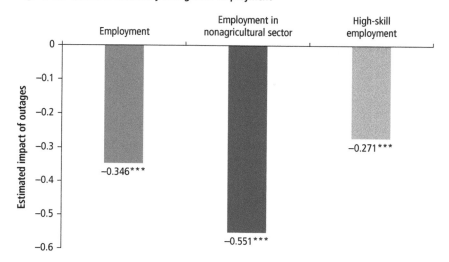

Source: Mensah 2018.
Note: The reported coefficients are of outages in a community using the instrumental variable regression approach.
*** $p < 0.01$.

BOX 4.6

Associations among Access, Quality of Service Provision, and Economic Outcomes

Using Multi-Tier Framework (MTF) data (2017) from Liberia and Ethiopia, this box shows the correlation between electricity uptake rate and the probability of an individual being employed in a nonfarm wage job.

The results in figure B4.6.1 clearly show a strong and positive association between uptake and employment in nonfarm cash-paying jobs. In other words, living in communities with high access rates increases the likelihood of having a cash-paying job in the nonfarm sector. This outcome provides suggestive evidence that the benefits of electrification increase when there is a high uptake rate.

Despite the above associations, this analysis argues strongly that the economic benefits are greater when service quality is high, that is, when the electricity supply can support productive uses rather than just lighting provision. Figure B4.6.2 shows a positive relationship between the share of households in the community with access to tiers 4 and 5 (see figure 4A.1) and the probability of employment in the nonfarm sector.

(continued next page)

BOX 4.6 (continued)

Figure B4.6.1 Densification and Employment

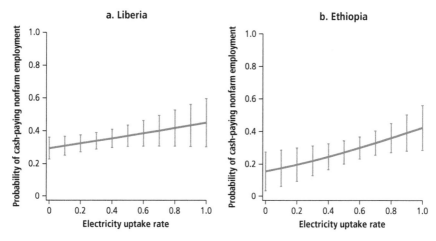

Source: Data from Multi-Tier Framework surveys in Liberia and Ethiopia 2017.
Note: Figures show correlation point estimates and their confidence intervals in vertical bars.

Figure B4.6.2 High Quality of Electricity Provision and Employment

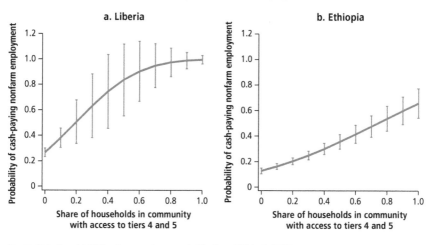

Source: Data from Multi-Tier Framework surveys in Liberia and Ethiopia 2017.
Note: Figures show correlation point estimates and their confidence intervals in vertical bars.

Outages Have Negative Implications for Public Finance in Africa

Aside from the impact on households and firms, the political economy impact of reliable electricity provision cannot be overstated. Studies have highlighted the impact of expanding electricity access on election outcomes in developing countries (Baskaran, Min, and Uppal 2015; Briggs 2012; Min 2015). This chapter shows that the provision of quality infrastructure services, such as reliable electricity, is a mechanism through which governments in developing countries can mobilize the tax revenues that are needed for development (Blimpo et al. 2018). On the one hand, connection to the grid can potentially signal government's commitment to the provision of social infrastructure and services and therefore reinforce the sense of an implicit fiscal pact between citizens and their government. On the other hand, the lack of access to such social infrastructure may engender protest actions in the form of refusal to pay taxes to the state because citizens judge the state incapable of honoring the fiscal pact.

Moreover, it is noteworthy that the quality of social infrastructure services matters as well, especially in urban areas. Poor-quality service delivery, such as incessant outages and brownouts, can be viewed as evidence of government incompetence and may suppress citizens' willingness to comply with tax regulations quasi-voluntarily. Evidence from the literature suggests that (quasi) public goods provision is at the heart of the fiscal pact between citizens and their respective governments (Bratton 2012; Timmons 2005; Timmons and Garfias 2015). As a result, the supply of public goods can induce positive attitudes among citizens toward honoring their tax obligations.

The impact of electricity reliability on taxation is likely to occur in two forms: the effect on citizens' incentives to pay taxes, and the tax revenue losses from the lost production associated with the negative impact of outages on the productive sectors of the economy (mainly industry).

Reliability and Tax Compliance Attitudes

Blimpo et al. (2018) estimate the effects of electricity access and reliability on the tax compliance attitudes of households in 36 countries in Africa. The results in figure 4.6 show that extending the grid to a community has a significant positive effect (statistically significant at the 10 percent level) on residents' attitudes toward paying taxes. The statistical effect becomes even stronger (5 percent level) when households' connection to grid electricity is considered. The study estimates the effects of reliability at the communal and household levels on tax compliance attitudes. Again, the results show the strong positive impact of access to reliable electricity on attitudes toward taxes.

In addition to the importance of access and reliability in explaining variations in tax compliance attitudes, this chapter argues that reliability plays a crucial role in sustainable economic growth and hence tax revenue mobilization. As shown by Allcott, Collard-Wexler, and O'Connell (2016), reliability affects firm performance and the overall growth of the productive sector. To this end,

Figure 4.6 Electricity Access, Reliability, and Tax Compliance Attitudes

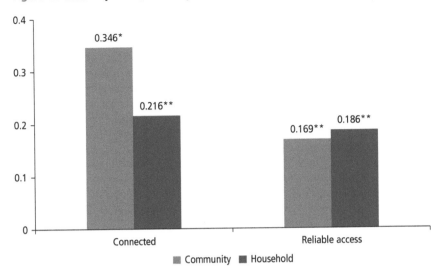

Source: Blimpo et al. 2018.
Note: The reported coefficients are of electricity access and reliability using the instrumental variable regression approach.
$** p < 0.05; * p < 0.1$.

this analysis further investigates the effect of reliability on tax compliance by decomposing the reliability measure into levels of reliability. This allows the relative importance of the various tiers of reliability for tax compliance to be disentangled. The results suggest that households connected to the grid network but without electricity have a lower incentive to pay taxes compared with unconnected households (figure 4.7); that is, the value of the electrical connection is in the ability to utilize the service associated with the connection. When households are connected but unable to use the service, they view it as a failure of the state to provide the needed service to ensure that they benefit from their investment in the connection. Accordingly, a low incentive to pay taxes can be viewed as one way of expressing their resentment to the state.

Connected households with a regular supply of electricity have favorable attitudes toward taxes relative to unconnected households. The level of impact increases with the degree of reliability of supply. These results suggest that factors such as power outages encourage negative public attitudes toward honoring tax obligations. Accordingly, citizens may use nonpayment of taxes as a form of protest action against poor service delivery on the part of the state and utility companies.

To what extent does the impact of reliability on tax compliance attitudes vary between rural and urban households? The results in figure 4.8 show statistically

Figure 4.7 Reliability and Tax Compliance Attitudes

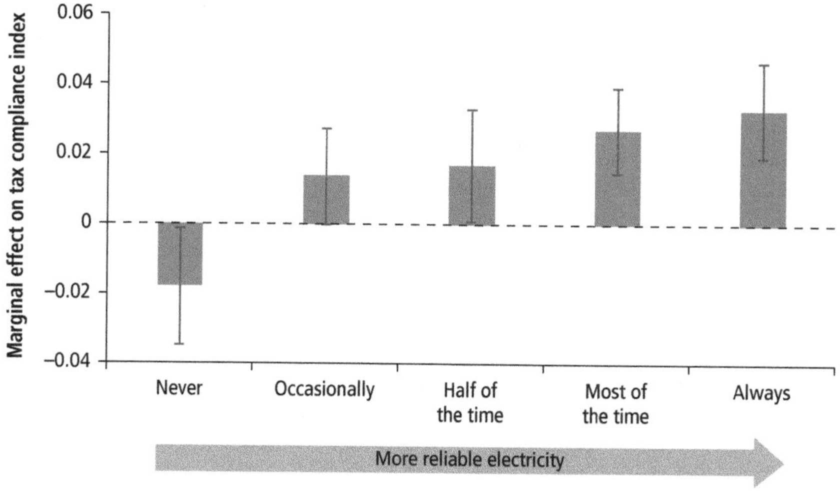

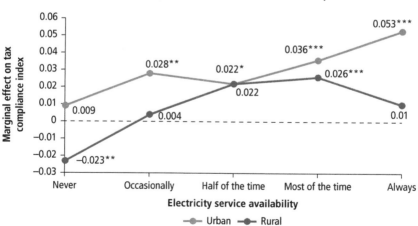

Source: Blimpo et al. 2018.
Note: The reported coefficients are marginal effects of a probit regression of reliability and attitudes toward taxes.

Figure 4.8 Reliability and Tax Compliance Attitudes: A Rural-Urban Perspective

Source: Blimpo et al. 2018.
Note: The reported coefficients are marginal effects of a probit regression of reliability and attitudes toward taxes.
*** $p < 0.01$; ** $p < 0.05$; * $p < 0.1$.

significant rural-urban differences in the effect of reliability on tax compliance. At each level of electricity provision, we observe a larger and statistically significant impact on tax compliance in urban areas relative to rural areas. The results provide suggestive evidence that reliability matters more for urban than for rural households in explaining individuals' attitudes toward honoring their tax obligations.

These pieces of evidence lead to the conclusion that reliability matters for tax revenue mobilization in Africa. Hence, as a strategy to encourage positive attitudes among citizens toward honoring their tax obligations, governments in the region can harness the benefits of reliable electricity provision.

Potential Tax Revenue Gains from Reliable Electricity

The evidence in the preceding section underscores the impact of reliable electricity provision on tax compliance attitudes. What are the implications of frequent electricity outages on the tax revenues of the governments in countries in Africa? What are the losses in tax revenue resulting from electricity shortages and their impacts on productive sectors?

Blimpo et al. (2018) quantify the potential tax revenue gains that could accrue to African governments from the complete elimination of electricity outages in their respective economies. However, the analysis is constrained by the lack of consistent and adequate data on the impact of reliability on households, as well as on households' income tax payments. Thus, the simulation is restricted to tax revenues associated with the industrial sector. The tax revenue gains from an improvement in the quality of electricity supply are simulated by estimating the present value of future tax revenue losses attributed to the effects of power outages on the industrial sector. The underlying reasoning is that the state loses significant tax revenue from the negative impacts of power outages on firms' revenues and profits. Accordingly, complete elimination of outages by fixing the problems of the power sector will, all else being equal, lead to tax revenue gains.

The exercise hypothesizes two potential channels through which outages affect tax payments from firms:

- First, outages lower the profitability of existing firms, thereby reducing tax payments.
- Second, electricity supply irregularities increase the expected cost of doing business and constrain the establishment of new firms, thereby stifling expansion of the tax base.

Exploring these channels under conservative assumptions, a simulation reveals that substantial tax revenue gains could potentially accrue to African economies from the provision of reliable grid electricity. On average, the simulation finds that Angola, Ghana, Kenya, Nigeria, and South Africa are potentially the highest gainers, with an increase of more than US$300 million in total

Figure 4.9 Simulated Tax Revenue Gains from the Provision of Reliable Electricity

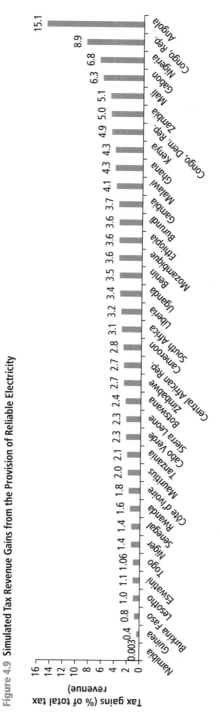

Source: Blimpo et al. 2018.

tax revenue each per year. Expressing these estimates in total tax revenues, Angola (15.1 percent), the Republic of Congo (8.9 percent), Nigeria (6.8 percent), Gabon (6.3 percent), and Mali (5.1 percent) are the top five countries in potential tax revenue gains (figure 4.9). Cumulatively, the estimated gains in the study countries are more than 4 percent of total tax revenue. It is important to emphasize that although these simulations do not account for the cost of resolving the problems of outages in the electricity sector, the magnitude of the potential revenue gains is indicative of the potential of reliable electricity provision in expanding the public purse in many countries in the region.

Conclusion

Although access to electricity is important, reliability is critical for magnifying the impact of access; poor quality imposes notable economic losses in Africa. Unreliability is high in many countries in the region. There is also high heterogeneity in reliability between firms and households. The extent of electricity reliability is unevenly distributed across economic and geographic groups. Electricity is more reliable in urban than in rural localities and among households in the upper-income quintiles relative to low-income households.

Reliability is an important driver of the uptake of electricity. Unreliable electricity supply in a community reduces the expected benefits of electricity, hence reducing the incentive of households to invest in electricity connections.

Unreliability has a strong negative impact on households, firms, and governments. For households, unreliable access has a negative impact on employment and income. The effects on firms are strong and myriad. Unreliability imposes a negative impact on firms' output, revenue, and productivity. There is also a negative impact on entrepreneurship and the rate of firm entry. The mechanisms through which unreliability affects these outcomes include a negative impact on trade and export competitiveness of firms, as well as reduced demand for skilled labor. For governments, unreliable electricity has a negative impact on public finance, particularly tax revenue mobilization. Unreliability reduces the tax compliance attitudes of citizens in the region and lowers tax revenues.

Overall, the evidence from the chapter suggests that reliability is paramount in every electricity network to maximize the gains from access. Reliability matters not only for the impact of access, but for uptake as well. To this end, electrification efforts in the region should focus on not only expanding access, but also improving reliability. Upgrading reliability would require sufficient investment in the maintenance of electricity infrastructure and reforming the sector to improve revenue collection by utilities. Additionally, in countries with well-demarcated industrial enclaves, priority might be given to industries during periods of power crises, given their economic importance.

Annex 4A: Estimation of the Impact of Electricity Outages on Firm Productivity and Output

Mensah (2018) estimates the causal effects of electricity outages on the output and productivity of firms in 23 countries in Africa. The analysis uses data from World Bank Enterprise Surveys between 2006 and 2015. The baseline equation for estimation of the impact is the following:

$$y_{kjdct} = \beta E_{kjdct} + \psi_j + \eta_c + \Lambda_{dt} + \varepsilon_{kjdct},$$

in which y_{kjdct} is the outcome variable (including value added, value added per worker, total factor productivity, and labor demand) for firm k in district j, industry d, country c, at time t; E_{kjdct} represents the electricity reliability experienced by the firm. The estimation includes district fixed effects, ψ_j, to control

Figure 4A.1 Multi-Tier Framework for Measuring Electricity Access

<table>
<tr><th colspan="3"></th><th>TIER 0</th><th>TIER 1</th><th>TIER 2</th><th>TIER 3</th><th>TIER 4</th><th>TIER 5</th></tr>
<tr><td rowspan="15">Attributes</td><td rowspan="5">1</td><td rowspan="5">Peak capacity</td><td rowspan="2">Power capacity ratings (in W or daily Wh)</td><td></td><td>Min 3 W</td><td>Min 50 W</td><td>Min 200 W</td><td>Min 800 W</td><td>Min 2 kW</td></tr>
<tr><td></td><td>Min 12 Wh</td><td>Min 200 Wh</td><td>Min 1.0 kWh</td><td>Min 3.4 kWh</td><td>Min 8.2 kWh</td></tr>
<tr><td rowspan="3">OR services</td><td></td><td rowspan="3">Lighting of 1,000 lmhr/day</td><td rowspan="3">Electrical lighting, air circulation, television, and phone charging are possible</td><td></td><td></td><td></td></tr>
<tr><td></td><td></td><td></td><td></td></tr>
<tr><td></td><td></td><td></td><td></td></tr>
<tr><td rowspan="2">2</td><td rowspan="2">Availability (duration)</td><td>Hours per day</td><td></td><td>Min 4 hrs</td><td>Min 4 hrs</td><td>Min 8 hrs</td><td>Min 16 hrs</td><td>Min 23 hrs</td></tr>
<tr><td>Hours per evening</td><td></td><td>Min 1 hr</td><td>Min 2 hrs</td><td>Min 3 hrs</td><td>Min 4 hrs</td><td>Min 4 hrs</td></tr>
<tr><td>3</td><td>Reliability</td><td></td><td></td><td></td><td></td><td></td><td>Max 14 disruptions per week</td><td>Max 3 disruptions per week of total duration <2 hrs</td></tr>
<tr><td>4</td><td>Quality</td><td></td><td></td><td></td><td></td><td></td><td colspan="2">Voltage problems do not affect the use of desired appliances.</td></tr>
<tr><td>5</td><td>Legality</td><td></td><td></td><td></td><td></td><td></td><td colspan="2">Bill is paid to the utility, prepaid cardseller, or authorized representative.</td></tr>
<tr><td>6</td><td>Health and safety</td><td></td><td></td><td></td><td></td><td></td><td colspan="2">Absence of past accidents and perception of high risk in the future.</td></tr>
</table>

Note: lmhr = lumen hours; kW = kilowatts; kWh = kilowatt hours; Max = maximum; Min = minimum; W = watts; Wh = watt hours.

for unobserved time-invariant differences across districts; industry-year fixed effects, Λ_{dt}, to absorb common shocks in the 2-digit industry in each year; and country fixed effects, η_c, to account for cross-country time-invariant differences.

Causal estimation of the impact of infrastructure services, such as the quality of electricity, is often beset with the challenge of endogeneity. For instance, the distribution and intensity of electricity outages are nonrandom across space and time. The presence of local economic, social, and political factors may confound the relationship between outages and the outcome variables of interest. Hence, an ordinary least squares estimation of the impact is likely to be biased. To overcome this challenge of identification, the instrumental variable approach is used by exploiting spatial and time variations in technical losses in the electricity network as an instrument for electricity outages.

Note

1. Direct exports refer to the share of firms' sales of output in foreign markets. Indirect exports are composed of the share of sales from output sold to domestic third-party firms that export the product.

References

Abeberese, A. B., C. Ackah, and P. Asuming. 2017. "Analysing the Extent and Sources of Productivity Losses from Electricity Shortages for Small and Medium-Sized Enterprises." Policy Brief 33305, International Growth Centre, London.

Adamba, C. 2018. "Effect of School Electrification on Learning Outcomes: A Subnational Level Analysis of Students' Pass Rate in English and Mathematics in Ghana." *Educational Research for Policy and Practice* 17 (1): 15–31.

Alby, P., J.-J. Dethier, and S. Straub. 2013. "Firms Operating under Electricity Constraints in Developing Countries." *World Bank Economic Review* 27 (1): 109–32. https://elibrary.worldbank.org/doi/abs/10.1093/wber/lhs018.

Allcott, H., A. Collard-Wexler, and S. D. O'Connell. 2016. "How Do Electricity Shortages Affect Industry? Evidence from India." *American Economic Review* 106 (3): 587–624.

Andersen, T., and C.-J. Dalgaard. 2013. "Power Outages and Economic Growth in Africa." *Energy Economics* 38 (July): 19–23.

Baskaran, T., B. Min, and Y. Uppal. 2015. "Election Cycles and Electricity Provision: Evidence from a Quasi-Experiment with Indian Special Elections." *Journal of Public Economics* 126 (June): 64–73.

Bensch, G., M. Kreibaum, T. Mbegalo, J. Peters, and N. Wagner. 2017. *The Status of Energy Access in Three Regions of Tanzania—Baseline Report for an Urban Grid Upgrading and Rural Extension Project*. Essen, Germany: RWI. http://www.rwi-essen.de/media/content/pages/publikationen/rwi-materialien/rwi-materialien_111.pdf.

Blimpo, M. P., J. T. Mensah, K. O. Opalo, and R. Shi. 2018. "Electricity Provision and Tax Mobilization in Africa." Policy Research Working Paper 8408, World Bank, Washington, DC.

Bratton, M. 2012. "Citizen Perceptions of Local Government Responsiveness in Sub-Saharan Africa." *World Development* 40 (3): 516–27.

Briggs, R. C. 2012. "Electrifying the Base? Aid and Incumbent Advantage in Ghana." *Journal of Modern African Studies* 50 (4): 603–24.

Burlando, A. 2014a. "Power Outages, Power Externalities, and Baby Booms." *Demography* 51 (4): 1477–500.

———. 2014b. "Transitory Shocks and Birth Weights: Evidence from a Blackout in Zanzibar." *Journal of Development Economics* 108 (May): 154–68.

Chakravorty, U., M. Pelli, and B. U. Marchand. 2014. "Does the Quality of Electricity Matter? Evidence from Rural India." *Journal of Economic Behavior and Organization* 107, Part A (November): 228–47.

Cole, M. A., R. J. Elliott, G. Occhiali, and E. Strobl. 2018. "Power Outages and Firm Performance in Sub-Saharan Africa." *Journal of Development Economics* 134 (September): 150–59.

Dasso, R., F. Fernandez, and H. Ñopo. 2015. "Electrification and Educational Outcomes in Rural Peru." Discussion Paper 8928, Institute of Labor Economics, Bonn.

Dutch Datacenter Association. 2017. "Economic Impact of Multi-Tenant Data Centers in the Netherlands." Dutch Datacenter Association, Amsterdam, Netherlands.

Eifert, B., A. Gelb, and V. Ramachandran. 2008. "The Cost of Doing Business in Africa: Evidence from Enterprise Survey Data." *World Development* 36 (9): 1531–46.

Fetzer, T., O. Pardo, and A. Shanghavi. 2018. "More Than an Urban Legend: The Long-Term Socio-Economic Effects of Unplanned Fertility Shocks." *Journal of Population Economics* 31 (4): 1125–76.

Fisher-Vanden, K., E. T. Mansur, and Q. Wang. 2015. "Electricity Shortages and Firm Productivity: Evidence from China's Industrial Firms." *Journal of Development Economics* 114 (May): 172–88. doi:https://doi.org/10.1016/j.jdeveco.2015.01.002.

Glanz, J. 2011. "Google Details, and Defends, Its Use of Electricity." *New York Times*, September 8.

Hardy, M., and J. McCasland. 2017. "Lights Off, Lights On: The Effects of Electricity Shortages on Small Firms." Unpublished. https://www.aeaweb.org/conference/2017/preliminary /paper/4Hsy6Zr8.

Lipscomb, M., A. Mobarak, and T. Barham. 2013. "Development Effects of Electrification: Evidence from the Topographic Placement of Hydropower Plants in Brazil." *American Economic Journal, Applied Economics* 5 (2): 200–31.

Marston, R. 2017. "Microsoft's Data Centre Investment to Boost SA Cloud Adoption." *IT News Africa*, June 12.

Melitz, M. J. 2003. "The Impact of Trade on Intra-Industry Reallocations and Aggregate Industry Productivity." *Econometrica* 71 (6): 1695–725.

Mensah, J. T. 2016. "Bring Back Our Light: Power Outages and Industrial Performance in Sub-Saharan Africa." Presented at the Annual Meeting of the Agricultural and Applied Economics Association, Boston, MA, July 31–August 2.

———. 2017. "Reliability Matters! Electricity Shortages and Firm Performance in Sub-Saharan Africa." Working Paper, Swedish University of Agricultural Sciences.

———. 2018. "Jobs! Electricity Shortages and Unemployment in Africa." Policy Research Working Paper 8415, World Bank, Washington, DC.

Min, B. 2015. *Power and the Vote: Elections and Electricity in the Developing World.* Cambridge, UK: Cambridge University Press.

Oyuke, A., P. Halley Penar, and B. Howard. 2016. "Off-Grid or 'Off-on': Lack of Access, Unreliable Electricity Supply Still Plague Majority of Africans." Dispatch 75, Afrobarometer.

Samad, H. A., and F. Zhang. 2016. *Benefits of Electrification and the Role of Reliability: Evidence from India.* Washington, DC: World Bank.

Steinbuks, J., and B. Foster. 2010. "When Do Firms Generate? Evidence on In-House Electricity Supply in Africa." *Energy Economics* 32 (3): 505–14.

Timmons, J. F. 2005. "The Fiscal Contract: States, Taxes, and Public Services." *World Politics* 57 (4): 530–67.

———, and F. Garfias. 2015. "Revealed Corruption, Taxation, and Fiscal Accountability: Evidence from Brazil." *World Development* 70 (June): 13–27.

Trimble, C., M. Kojima, I. Perez Arroyo, and F. Mohammadzadeh. 2016. "Financial Viability of Electricity Sectors in Sub-Saharan Africa: Quasi-Fiscal Deficits and Hidden Costs." Policy Research Working Paper 7788, World Bank, Washington, DC.

Uptime Institute. 2012. *Data Center Site Infrastructure Tier Standard: Topology.* New York: Uptime Institute.

Verhoogen, E. A. 2008. "Trade, Quality Upgrading, and Wage Inequality in the Mexican Manufacturing Sector." *Quarterly Journal of Economics* 123 (2): 489–530.

Chapter 5

Electricity Plus: Leveraging Complementary Factors for Impact

Necessary but Often Not Sufficient

The electrification of Sub-Saharan Africa (hereafter Africa or SSA) should be treated as a necessity and not solely based on the measurement of short-term impacts. More insight into other factors that need to come together for the impact to be more substantial and more quickly realized is required.

With electrification, business opportunities become available for micro-, small, and medium-sized enterprises in such areas as hairdressing, eating establishments, and tailoring. Impacts rise in the medium term as complementary factors are introduced and households and businesses adjust to electricity's potential. Education and health outcomes may improve through the electrification of schools and clinics. Economic impacts grow as electricity becomes increasingly available as a strategic input for industries and services. In the long term, this results in improved human development and the transformation of SSA economies. The pace and degree of these impacts depend on the initial conditions and the speed with which complementary factors are put in place.

Africa's electrification cannot be dissociated from complementary factors that help realize its impact. The mix of complementary factors differs across countries, and even within countries, it may present different opportunities. Some of these factors may take time to fall into place for the benefit to be fully realized. Therefore, the planning perspective needs to be oriented to the longer-term buildup of the economy.

Considerable economic literature has sought to measure the impact of electricity access in various contexts. At the macroeconomic level, regional and national studies find positive effects on growth, productivity, and employment. Studies find that power infrastructure has a significant effect on long-run growth in Africa (for example, Estache, Speciale, and Veredas 2005), with a similar relationship at the national level in Nigeria (Ayogu 1999). Escribano, Guasch, and Pena (2009) report that the quality of electricity has a significant impact on total factor productivity in 26 countries analyzed in Africa. A study of manufacturing sectors in 11 African nations finds that electricity triggered employment growth of about 2 percent (Goedhuys and Sleuwaegen 2010). Other studies find little, if any, impact from electricity alone, asserting that electrification needs to be accompanied by roads, research and development, and other elements to achieve productivity gains (Mayer-Tasch, Mukherjee, and Reiche 2013).

At the micro level, impacts are found in education, health, and women's empowerment, to name a few. Education benefits through the ability of schools to stay open longer and use electronics, such as computers, which tends to help retain teachers and attract students.[1] Household lighting allows students to study at home (IEG 2008). Improvements in health accrue from several areas, including electricity for clinics, cleaner household air from reduced use of charcoal or biomass for lighting and cooking (Hutton et al. 2006), better health knowledge through increased access to television, and refrigeration of food and medicine. Women benefit from electrification because it facilitates the household chores they perform in many countries. Electricity also increases empowerment by expanding female access to mass media (Haves 2012) and generating employment opportunities (Dinkelman 2011).

The variation in the measured impacts sometimes opens a debate among experts and policy makers on the necessity of electrification in lower-income countries. However, this debate misses the fundamental point that electricity is only one of the critical factors that need to interact efficiently to provide a conducive environment for boosting firm performance and the welfare of households. Accordingly, it is not surprising that the findings vary in different contexts, including the time elapsed since electrification.

The impact of electricity access is conditioned on the availability of other services, referred to herein as *complementary factors*. The central policy issue is not only to quantify the impact of electrification on the economy; more importantly, it is to identify the conditions under which the impact is more likely to be larger.

This chapter emphasizes the need to accompany electrification efforts with complementary factors and investments that would foster modern economic activities. It explores the literature and uses newly available Multi-Tier Framework (MTF) survey data from the World Bank to provide direction on the types of complementary factors that are associated with significant impacts from electricity access.

Figure 5.1 illustrates the chapter's conceptual framework. It depicts electricity access as a necessary input to modern economic activities that are conducive to higher productivity and income growth. However, realization

Figure 5.1 **Economic Potential and Electricity**

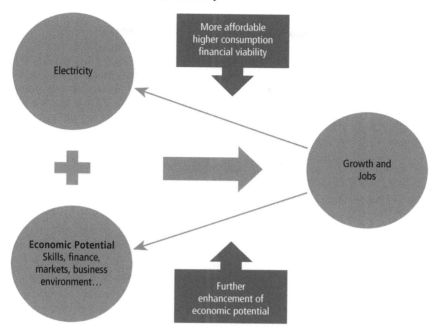

of the impact requires the presence of other necessary conditions, labeled under the broader term *economic potential*. Those conditions could include various levels of skills, access to finance, the business environment, and access to markets. These factors differ from one country to another, and they may vary among regions in a country. When the right combination of the necessary conditions is in place, electrification will lead to more growth and job creation, which, in turn, will feed back into higher usage and better economic potential.

This chapter addresses these questions and provides policy direction by first exploring the literature on the impact of electrification in different contexts to identify facilitating factors. It assesses the conditions under which significant impacts are found, including reports of heterogeneous effects, and draws lessons from the Integrated Rural Development (IRD) strategy that dominated development policy in the 1970s and 1980s. Second, the chapter uses newly available MTF data to analyze the relationship between the economic impact of electricity access and the presence of other factors, including the level of human capital, other physical infrastructure, public services, and economic opportunities. The complementary factors are likely to be more present in areas where people are already better off, and in urban centers and industrial zones. This presents challenges for the pursuit of inclusive growth: How can higher value added in the economy be achieved without excluding the vulnerable and the poor? It is equally important to view this analysis not only as a means for targeting the provision of electricity, but also, and more importantly, as a way to think about building up deprived areas by providing complementary factors along with electrification. Third, the chapter presents qualitative evidence from Senegal on the nexus between electrification and income-generating activities, including in rural contexts.

Drivers of Electricity Impact: What Can We Learn from the Literature?

The literature has largely focused on quantifying the impact of electricity access in different contexts. It provides little guidance on the conditions under which the impact may be realized. Some studies address this question, often not through analysis but rather in discussing and rationalizing the findings or lack thereof.

Significant methodological challenges to evaluating the impact of electrification arise because of self-selection. Wealthier households are more likely to connect to the grid. Therefore, a raw correlation between electricity access and income is expected to show a positive association without an indication of the extent to which electricity contributed to the outcome.

The considerable variation in the measured impact of electricity on economic activities may reflect this challenge in part. Such variation, however, can be counterproductive to sound policy formulation, given that many papers can support arguments one way or the other.

Evidence from Recent Systematic Reviews

Systematic reviews are one way to synthesize research findings and guide policy. Recent efforts by the World Bank's Independent Evaluation Group, the International Initiative for Impact Evaluation, and the Inter-American Development Bank have produced such reviews. However, even the systematic reviews come to varying conclusions, and they provide little guidance on the conditions under which the impacts may be realized.

Knox, Daccache, and Hess (2013) report limited evidence of the impacts of electricity infrastructure on agricultural productivity and poverty outcomes. Mathur, Oliver, and Tripney (2015) suggest that electricity access has an overall positive impact on household income in the farm and nonfarm sectors.

Jimenez (2017) finds that electricity access yields substantial gains in education, labor, and income, especially for women and small firms.

Knox, Daccache, and Hess (2013) examine the impacts of infrastructure investments, including electricity access, on agricultural productivity and poverty reduction. In their review, studies on Africa account for less than 10 percent of the countries examined. They conclude that there is limited evidence of the impacts of electricity infrastructure on agricultural productivity and poverty outcomes. Nevertheless, of the 16 percent of the studies that examine these outcomes, 40 percent find positive and significant effects of electricity infrastructure on agricultural productivity and poverty outcomes. The evidence is dominated by the impacts on poverty outcomes.

Mathur, Oliver, and Tripney (2015) conduct a systematic review of the impact of electricity on health, education, and welfare, including 51 studies in 24 countries on 3 continents, among them 14 African countries. The review shows that electricity access has positive and significant impacts on educational outcomes (study time, years of schooling, and school enrollment), with higher impacts for rural areas compared with urban areas. On income generation, the pooled estimate effect suggests that electricity access has an overall positive impact on household income in the farm and nonfarm sectors. Finally, they find that evidence of the impacts of electricity on health, women's empowerment, income, and firms' profits is thin, suggesting that more research is needed in those areas.

More recently, in a review of 50 impact evaluation studies published between 1986 and 2015, Jimenez (2017) reviews the literature on the impact of electricity across four continents (Africa, North America, South America, and Asia). The review includes 14 studies on Africa. It finds substantial gains from electricity for education, labor, and income, especially for women and small firms. However, the magnitudes of the impacts vary across studies, with many of them finding nonsignificant effects. Jimenez (2017) suggests that the lack of large effects might be due to short-term exposure to electricity. The review shows that more than 64 percent of the impact evaluations are based on one year of exposure to electricity, making it difficult to observe the gains of electrification, which often take time to develop.

Although this literature can provide information about the value of electricity, it offers little policy guidance on how to be more efficient in placing energy access within the broader development agenda.

Evidence from Recent Research in Africa
Some recent studies overcome major methodological hurdles to provide some evidence of causal effects. First, Dinkelman (2011) examines the impacts of rural electrification in South Africa and finds that electricity access increases

employment, with a specific impact on women's labor market participation. The findings suggest that, in that context, perhaps strengthening women's capacity and access to productive assets may lead to effects that are more significant. More recently, based on an experimental study in Kenya, Lee, Miguel, and Wolfram (2016) find no effect stemming from exogenous access to grid electricity. They estimate a negative net welfare effect under a set of assumptions. Although the paper does not analyze complementarities directly, it argues that missing complementary factors could justify the findings (for example, credit constraints or existing infrastructure). Chaplin et al. (2017) evaluate Millennium Corporation Challenge–funded grid extension programs on a wide range of outcomes. The study reports overall modest impacts, with significant uptake among businesses as well as an increase in the share of households operating income-generating activities that use grid electricity. A notable finding is the 34 percent increase in land values.

In rural Rwanda, Lenz et al. (2017) demonstrate that the impacts of electricity on business activities are most visible in communities that already had thriving commerce before electrification. Similarly, based on a representative sample of informal firms in seven West African cities, Grimm, Hartwig, and Lay (2013) show that electricity access exerts a positive impact on micro and small enterprises (MSEs) in the highest profit quintile. This finding suggests that MSEs might have to pass a critical threshold to benefit from the positive effects of electricity access. Moreover, the study finds that MSEs that are not constrained by credit benefit from electricity access, suggesting that credit might be a complementary factor for reaping the benefits from electricity access.

Grimm, Hartwig, and Lay (2013) find no systematic evidence that electricity access increases the performance of MSEs. There is a clear and decisive positive impact on the clothing sector, which seems to be the most homogeneous sector. The paper highlights the need to account for the heterogeneity of the informal sector. For the more homogeneous sample of informal tailors in Ouagadougou, Burkina Faso, the paper finds a positive influence of access to electricity on MSE performance by promoting the uptake of modern machinery and business operations. For the subsample of tailors, the paper finds that electricity access significantly increases working hours and possession of electric sewing machines. Similarly, Peters, Sievert, and Vance (2013) show a positive joint effect of electricity connection and usage of business development services and micro-credit in peri-urban areas in Ghana.

Several qualitative studies explore the complementarities explicitly. Bernard (2010) reviews the literature on rural electrification over the past 30 years in Africa. The author recognizes that although the development paradigms of rural electrification programs have evolved significantly, the impacts of electricity access remain mostly undocumented and low. He points out that, to avoid the failure experienced by previous rural electrification programs, electricity must be seen as an input among others in development projects. Limited productive use of electricity in Africa reduces households' ability to engage in electrification projects. Similarly, Kirubi (2006) examines the impacts of modern energy on productive activities in rural Kenya (Mpeketoni village). According to the author, access to electricity in combination with simultaneous access to markets and other infrastructure (roads, communication, and schools) contributed to the robust growth of micro-enterprises in clear and compelling ways.

In a broader review, focusing on the African context and productive use of electricity (PRODUSE), a joint study by the German Federal Enterprise for International Cooperation and the Energy Sector Management Assistance Program (Mayer-Tasch, Mukherjee, and Reiche 2013) highlights the impacts of electricity access on micro-enterprises and small firms. The PRODUSE study shows that the manufacturing and services sectors use electricity mostly for lighting and phone charging, and the uptake of electric appliances remains modest. Although such use of electricity might affect production, the impact on productivity and profits might be limited. The evidence provided by the PRODUSE study points out the absence of facilitating factors such as sensitization, access to finance, public infrastructure, and business development services. All of those complementary factors are highly recommended by the PRODUSE study to maximize the impacts of electricity access, especially in Africa.

Implementation, Sequencing, and Context Specificity: Lessons from Integrated Rural Development

This report calls for a rethinking of electrification policies, from "stand-alone" to a more coordinated approach in which the provision of electrification is complemented with basic infrastructure and access to social services. The provision of electricity should be accompanied by elements such as market access, financial services, and public services to ensure that the various segments of the local economy function efficiently to engender development. For example, an agro-processing firm that secures access to electricity will still require access to markets and finance to create jobs.

This line of thought may resemble the IRD strategy that dominated development policy in the 1970s and 1980s. The IRD concept grew from development practitioners' realization that despite the considerable development assistance for agriculture, productivity remained relatively low because of constraints and frictions in the rural economy. As a result, IRD aimed to deal simultaneously with constraints in the agriculture and nonagriculture sectors, including but not limited to health, education, access to markets, and infrastructure (Baah-Dwomoh 2016; Paul 1998; Qadeer, Rashid, and Babar 1977; Ruttan 1984). However, the IRD policies failed to yield the desired outcomes because of factors such as project complexity, a one-size-fits-all philosophy, lack of local participation, and an unfavorable economic and political environment, among other reasons (Baah-Dwomoh 2016; Chase and Wilkinson 2015).

There are significant differences between the notion of identifying binding constraints and addressing them. First, this report does not advocate a "one-size-fits-all" strategy that ignores inter- and within-country heterogeneity. On the contrary, the report requires more context-specific research to guide policy with more precision.

Second, thinking of electrification as a necessary condition for modern economic activities means that there need not be simultaneity in the investment. It instead suggests that sequencing is welcomed but should be informed by analysis of complementary factors to determine the right sequence or packages of interventions.

Third, investments in complementary factors need not be addressed across the board and in all communities. The private sector, when given the right incentives, can play an essential role in providing ancillary investments and services that will complement the provision of electricity for more significant impacts.

The current Anchor Business Community model in rural electrification is a good example on which to build, to promote further impact by engaging the private sector in the provision of complementary factors as well as investment in electrification. Anchor Business Community is a business model of electrification in which electricity companies leverage *anchor* customers to reduce the financial risk of extending electricity to rural communities where demand is likely to be low and uncertain (Givens 2016). In this framework, the electricity provider identifies an anchor customer with high demand for electricity to ensure the financial viability of electricity provision, local businesses with demand for electricity for productive uses, and community households with demand for basic energy services. The model has been piloted in Kabunyata village, in the Luwero district of Uganda, where a telecommunications company was identified as the anchor customer. A solar generator set was provided to supply electricity to the mobile telecommunication tower as well as to extend power to households and small businesses in the village (Kurz 2014).

Identifying Complementary Factors: Evidence from the MTF Data

The World Bank Enterprise Surveys report issues that firms identify as major constraints to their operations and growth. Figure 5.2 uses the most recent survey for Sub-Saharan African countries[2] to assess the issues that firms reported

Figure 5.2 **Share of Firms That Reported the Listed Factor as a Major Constraint, among Firms Not Listing Electricity as a Constraint**

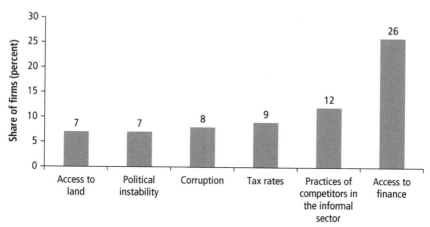

Source: Adapted from the World Bank Enterprise Survey.

as major constraints, focusing on firms that did not report electricity as a constraint. Access to finance and credit constraints stand out, by far, as the number one constraint.

The analysis considers two outcome variables: the prevalence of nonfarm, wage-paying jobs, and a measure of household income per person. The employment variable is a dummy that takes the value one if any member of the household holds a wage-paying job in the nonfarm sector.

As discussed in chapter 4, access to electricity services should emphasize the importance of reliability. In this analysis, access to electricity, or the variable capturing electricity, means access to reliable electricity. The variable measuring *electricity access* is designed to capture the reliability and availability of electricity service at the community and household levels. The variable captures the share of households who are in access tiers 4 or 5 (per the MTF classification; see figures 3.17 and 4A.1), the seasonal variation in the quality level of electricity access in the community, the number of unexpected outages of street lights, the duration of the outages, and a subjective assessment of the extent to which the residents are satisfied with grid services.

Based on an exploration of the literature, the analysis focuses on four potential complementary factors:

- First, the variable *access to market* measures the existence of a market locally or access to an outside market in which to sell goods and services. It captures the size of the local market, access to the nearest city by vehicle at all times during the year, the presence of bus service, distance to the district head-quarters or nearest city, and the extent to which the community has mobile signal coverage.

- Second, the variable *access to credit* aims to measure the extent to which members of the community can borrow funds to finance economic activities. Because of data limitations, proxies are used that may not ade-quately capture this primary goal. The variable combines the existence of banking services in the community (rural bank, micro-credit institution, or credit union) and the share of households whose head has a bank account.

- Third, the variable *skills* is an index that captures the average skill level within a community, which may be indicative of the ability to exploit various entre-preneurial activities. It captures the share of the population with at least secondary education and the presence of secondary or technical and voca-tional schools.

- Finally, *access to public services* in the community can also play a pivotal complementary role to entrepreneurial initiatives. Although red tape in the public administration is often recognized as an impediment to busi-ness activities, in many parts of a country, especially in rural areas, many public services do not even exist. The variable captures the existence within the community of formal childcare services, a primary school, a health clinic, a post office, a police station, and agricultural extension services.

Exploration of Complementary Factors: Evidence from Rwanda

Data from Rwanda suggest that skills and access to a market have amplifying effects on nonfarm job creation, whereas access to a market, access to credit, and access to public services matter more for income generation. Here, income can come from nonformal jobs; hence, there is a difference between wage-paying jobs and income generation broadly (table 5.1).

Table 5.1 **Impacts of Electricity: The Role of Complementary Factors**

Complementary factors (conditional on having reliable electricity)	Wage employment in the nonfarm sector	Household income
Access to markets	+	+
Skills	+	No
Public services	No	+
Access to credit	No	+

Source: Estimations using Multi-Tier Framework data for Rwanda 2017.
Note: + denotes positive and statistically significant effects.

As expected, the analysis provides evidence that complementary factors matter to maximizing the impact of electricity access for income generation and wage employment in the nonfarm sector. For both outcomes, access to markets increases the benefit of access to electricity. The findings suggest that access to markets might increase the potential for business development because it guarantees the interaction between production and demand. Conditional on having reliable electricity, a higher level of skills increases the likelihood of employment in the nonfarm sector. Similarly, public services and access to credit favor income generation in the presence of reliable electricity. Both factors might be seen as a way to increase the opportunity for income generation for households.

Figure 5.3 shows the marginal effects of access to reliable electricity, conditional on the levels of complementary factors. In each panel, the vertical red line represents the median value of the facilitating factor variable. The horizontal red line refers to the nonsignificant level of the marginal effects. As can be seen, high values of the index of complementary factors increase the marginal effect of access to reliable electricity on income generation and wage employment in the nonfarm sector.

Figure 5.3 Marginal Effects of Access to Reliable Electricity Conditional on Facilitating Factors

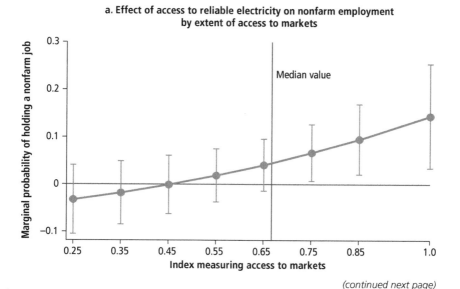

a. Effect of access to reliable electricity on nonfarm employment by extent of access to markets

(continued next page)

Figure 5.3 (continued)

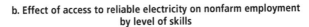

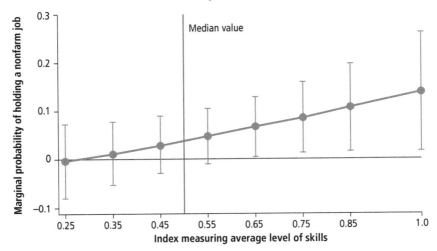

b. Effect of access to reliable electricity on nonfarm employment by level of skills

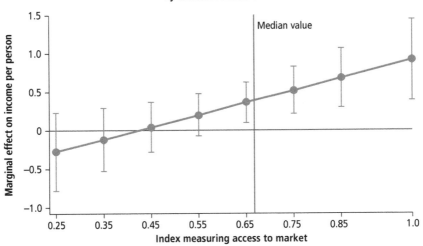

c. Effect of access to reliable electricity on household income by extent of access to market

(continued next page)

Figure 5.3 (continued)

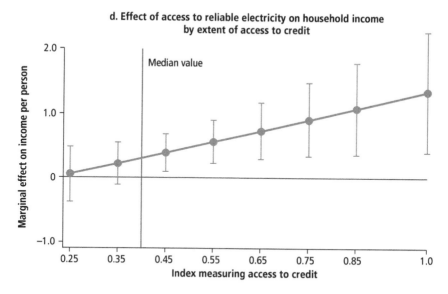

Source: Estimations using Multi-Tier Framework data for Rwanda 2017.

Three main policy implications can be drawn from the analysis of Rwanda. First, for larger impacts, electrification projects should ensure that communities have access to markets. Second, improving the accessibility of communities through better quality of public infrastructure (for example, transport such as roads and railways) will allow communities to take advantage of electrification, especially in rural areas. Third, investment in skills is needed to ensure job creation outside the nonfarm sector and stimulate transformation of the economy.

Demand for Electricity for Income-Generating Activities: Qualitative Evidence from Rural Senegal

A qualitative investigation in rural Senegal showed that households primarily view access to electricity as a means to enhance their economic livelihoods. However, to achieve this goal requires skills training, access to credit, and a market in which to sell their products.

To gauge the importance of electrification for income generation and the priorities of households, a qualitative investigation was conducted in several countries, including communities in rural areas in Senegal. Two predominantly agricultural villages (Ndeuge and Mbissao) were included. Electricity poles were present throughout the village of Ndeuge, although the village was not covered by the grid. The village chief reported that the poles were put in place 13 years ago because of the imminent arrival of the electrical grid, but it never materialized. The village chief uses a car battery to power his small television, to charge his mobile phone, and for lighting. With respect to affordability, the village chief stated he recently paid an electricity bill of CFAF 120,000 (about US$220) to the utility. He reported that a former mayor obtained grid electrical connections for his home village, which is not far from Ndeuge. The residents of Ndeuge and surrounding areas combined financial resources to obtain electricity from that village to their farms (not their residences). The electricity is used to pump water on their farms during the dry season; the water is used for onion production, helping them generate revenue.

The community of Ndeuge recently approached the national electricity company, Senelec, to get an estimate for connecting more farms. The electricity company estimated the connection costs to be approximatively CFAF 15 million (about US$27,300). Although the community members did not at the time have the financial resources required, they reported a strong commitment to connect to the grid when possible.

Compared with the village of Ndeuge, the story of Mbissao is similar but in reverse order. The government brought electricity to the community, and many households are connected. Three neighboring villages joined their efforts to collect the necessary collateral to borrow CFAF 64 million (about US$116,500) to expand the power grid to their farms. Credit Mutuel du Senegal granted the loan at an interest rate of 12 percent for two years. The villages have already repaid close to 80 percent of the loan. A flood interrupted their activities for five months, and they have fallen behind in repayment, which has increased their interest rate to 25 percent. Interestingly, they are not worried about the repayment. After repaying this loan, they plan to take another loan for other income-generating activities, such as breeding animals.

Both villages (Ndeuge and Mbissao) needed electricity that could help them generate income. However, had they not been able to access credit and proper training, the villages would not have been able to seize the opportunity. Identifying and supporting communities like this may prove to be the best way to expand electrification in a financially viable way while achieving the development goal of job creation and inclusive growth.

Beyond Lighting: Solar Off-Grid Solutions Should Primarily Target Economic Livelihoods

Off-grid solutions to electricity access have generated hope for many communities to gain access much faster. However, off-grid solutions have mainly focused on lighting and charging cell phones. There is a need to shift more toward the enhancement of economic livelihoods.

A team of researchers from Columbia University analyzed the experiences of a few hundred energy customers in Uganda and Mali. The customers were provided with 24/7 solar power for an extended period at market cost. Five years later, the researchers found that household energy consumption had grown about fourfold. However, for a subset of households that used electricity for income-generating activities (between 5 and 10 percent of the households), the consumption of electricity had grown by 10 to 20 times over the same period. Underlying this experiment was the researchers' view that energy access should mean "a situation where you want to use power when you want to use it, and only pay for what you use."[3] The challenge is whether one could identify and support those entrepreneurs up front and incorporate that into electrification planning. These are areas in which research can inform policy makers.

These "shared solar" plants are a modular micro-grid solution providing electricity to a cluster of customers who are not presently considered viable for grid connectivity. This solution has allowed people to start income-generating businesses. The technology has been in operation in Mali, Uganda, and Bolivia since 2010, 2011, and 2013, respectively. Another finding from this research shows that energy consumption steadily grew over these years. Consumption, which started at US$2.5 per household per month in 2011, escalated to nearly US$10 in 2013. These findings suggest strong household willingness to pay as incomes rise. The researchers contend, however, that given the capacity and current level of solar technology, generating high-productivity activities going forward would require grid electricity.

The results of the Columbia University study indicate off-grid electrification can offer economic opportunities to rural communities. Another good example is an investment in off-grid solar electricity to pump water for irrigation in Gabbar, Senegal (box 5.1). Every household that used solar was willing to pay US$0.50/kilowatt and use it to raise high-value crops like onions and carrots. The solar energy would not have been financially viable if households were using it for rice or lower-value crops.

BOX 5.1

Solar Electricity and Off-Season Farming: The Experience of Gabbar, Senegal

Gabbar, Senegal, is one of the communities that benefited from a Columbia University experiment. The residents set up a management committee to ensure that the solar installations would be well run and serve the community. Members of the committee reported high satisfaction with the technology and significant changes in their livelihoods. One of those changes was that many no longer farm during the rainy season with all the drudgery that it engenders, including the unpredictability of the rains. They instead pump water and farm off-season with much more control.

The community reported paying a certain amount of their revenue into an account that is used to pay for maintenance and an employee to monitor the installations. The additional resources generated were to be used for projects to benefit the whole community, including residents without farms. The hope was that the technology could be expanded, given that access was granted to only 21 families. They planned to use their savings to acquire additional systems to serve their neighbors who were left out. They appointed those without access to manage the proceeds. The fact that outsiders selected those who would have access helped avoid conflicts, although there is a sense of guilt toward those who were not included. They all contributed land and labor (for example, digging) to set up the system.

Challenges with the technology arose, however. Each field had an oil-fed generator for backup, to supply water in the morning before sunrise. Even up to 10 a.m., solar energy was able to irrigate only two of the seven farms. However, use of the generator was much more expensive than solar. Another challenge was maintenance in the event of a breakdown. When the fuse broke down, it took one week to repair because of the need to bring a new one all the way from Dakar and identify the proper technician from outside to come and fix it. If the same thing were to happen today, it would take less time because some people in the community are being trained to fix minor problems. However, it may still take days, and the crop cannot go without water for long without a significant impact on productivity.

Conclusion

The literature focusing on quantifying the impact of electricity access is often context specific and depends on the extent to which electricity is the only or a more significant binding constraint to economic activity. The central policy question is not only to quantify the impacts of electrification on the economy, but more importantly to identify the conditions under which the impacts are more likely to be larger. Future research should aim at identifying minimal complementary factors in various contexts.

Notes

1. A study on Honduran schools finds that school enrollment dropped as a result of new employment opportunities created by electrification (Squires 2015).
2. The countries included are Angola (2010), Benin (2009), Botswana (2010), Burkina Faso (2009), Burundi (2014), Cameroon (2009), Cabo Verde (2009), the Central African Republic (2011), Chad (2009), the Democratic Republic of Congo (2013), the Republic of Congo (2009), Côte d'Ivoire (2009), Djibouti (2013), Eritrea (2009), Eswatini (2006), Ethiopia (2015), Gabon (2009), The Gambia (2006), Ghana (2013), Guinea (2006), Guinea-Bissau (2006), Kenya (2013), Lesotho (2009), Liberia (2009), Malawi (2014), Mali (2010), Mauritania (2014), Mauritius (2009), Mozambique (2008), Namibia (2014), Niger (2009), Nigeria (2014), Rwanda (2011), Senegal (2014), Sierra Leone (2007), South Africa (2007), South Sudan (2014), Sudan (2014), Tanzania (2013), Togo (2009), Uganda (2013), Zambia (2013), and Zimbabwe (2011).
3. Center for Global Development, Public Events, "Energy for Economic Prosperity: A Conversation with Donald Kaberuka and the Energy Access Targets Working Group," https://www.cgdev.org/event/energy-economic-prosperity-conversation -donald-kaberuka-and-energy-access-targets-working.

References

Ayogu, M. 1999. "Before Prebendalism: A Positive Analysis of Core Infrastructure Investment in a Developing Fiscal Federalism." *African Development Review* 11 (2): 169–98.

Baah-Dwomoh, J. K. 2016. Background paper for *African Transformation Report 2016: Transforming Africa's Agriculture*. Integrated Rural Development in Africa. Washington, DC: JICA Research Institute, Japan International Cooperation Agency.

Bernard, T. 2010. "Impact Analysis of Rural Electrification Projects in Sub-Saharan Africa." *World Bank Research Observer* 27 (1): 33–51.

Chaplin, D. A., A. Mamun, A. Protik, J. Schurrer, D. Vohra, K. Bos, H. Burak, L. Meyer, A. Dumitrescu, C. Ksoll, and T. Cook. 2017. "Grid Electricity Expansion in Tanzania by MCC: Findings from a Rigorous Impact Evaluation." Millennium Challenge Corporation, Princeton, NJ.

Chase, S., and E. Wilkinson. 2015. "What Happened to Integrated Rural Development?" The Hunger Project, Washington, DC. https://advocacy.thp.org/2015/08/11 /what-happened-to-integrated-rural-development.

Dinkelman, T. 2011. "The Effects of Rural Electrification on Employment: New Evidence from South Africa." *American Economic Review* 101 (7): 3078–108. http://www .aeaweb.org/articles.php?doi=10.1257/aer.101.7.3078.

Escribano, A., J. L. Guasch, and J. Pena. 2010. "Assessing the Impact of Infrastructure Quality on Firm Productivity in Africa: Cross-Country Comparisons Based on Investment." Policy Research Working Paper 5191, World Bank, Washington, DC.

Estache, A., B. Speciale, and D. Veredas. 2005. "How Much Does Infrastructure Matter to Growth in Sub-Saharan Africa?" World Bank, Washington, DC.

Givens, R. 2016. "The Anchor-Business-Community Model for Rural Energy Development: Is It a Viable Option?" Master's thesis, Duke University, Durham, NC.

Goedhuys, M., and L. Sleuwaegen. 2010. "High-Growth Entrepreneurial Firms in Africa: A Quantile Regression Approach." *Small Business Economics* 34 (1): 31–51.

Grimm, M., R. Hartwig, and J. Lay. 2013. "Electricity Access and the Performance of Micro and Small Enterprises: Evidence from West Africa." *European Journal of Development Research* 25 (5): 815–29.

Haves, E. 2012. "Does Energy Access Help Women? Beyond Anecdotes: A Review of the Evidence." Report, Ashden, London.

Hutton, G., E. Fehfuess, F. Tediosi, and S. Weiss. 2006. *Evaluation of the Costs and Benefits of Household Energy and Health Interventions at Global and Regional Levels.* Geneva: World Health Organization.

IEG (Independent Evaluation Group). 2008. *The Welfare Impact of Rural Electrification: A Reassessment of the Costs and Benefits.* Washington, DC: World Bank.

Jimenez, R. 2017. "Development Effects of Rural Electrification." IDB Policy Brief, Inter-American Development Bank, Washington, DC.

Kirubi, C. 2006. "How Important Is Modern Energy for Microenterprises? Evidence from Rural Kenya." Master's thesis, University of California, Berkeley. http://rael.berkeley.edu/files/2006/Kirubi-MS-Paper-2006.pdf.

Knox, J., A. Daccache, and T. Hess. 2013. "What Is the Impact of Infrastructural Investments in Roads, Electricity, and Irrigation on Agricultural Productivity?" CEE Review 11-007, Collaboration for Environmental Evidence. https://assets.publishing.service.gov.uk/media/57a08a0840f0b652dd00051a/CEE11-007_SystematicReview.pdf.

Kurz, K. 2014. "The ABC-Modell Anchor Customers as Core Clients for Mini-Grids in Emerging Economies." German Federal Enterprise for International Cooperation, Berlin.

Lee, K., E. Miguel, and C. Wolfram. 2016. "Appliance Ownership and Aspirations among Electric Grid and Home Solar Households in Rural Kenya." Working Paper 21949, National Bureau of Economic Research, Cambridge, MA.

Lenz, L., A. Munyehirwe, J. Peters, and M. Sievert. 2017. "Does Large-Scale Infrastructure Investment Alleviate Poverty? Impacts of Rwanda's Electricity Access Roll-Out Program." *World Development* 89 (January): 88–110.

Mathur, K., S. Oliver, and J. Tripney. 2015. "Access to Electricity for Improving Health, Education, and Welfare in Low- and Middle-Income Countries: A Systematic Review." The Campbell Collaboration, Oslo.

Mayer-Tasch, L., M. Mukherjee, and K. Reiche, eds. 2013. *Productive Use of Energy–PRODUSE: Measuring Impacts of Electrification on Small and Micro-Enterprises in Sub-Saharan Africa. Energy Sector Management Assistance Program.* Eschborn, Germany: Deutsche Gesellschaft für Internationale Zusammenarbeit (GIZ) GmbH. https://www.esmap.org/sites/esmap.org/files/ESMAP_GIZ_BMZ_AEI_PRODUSE_Study_FullText_Optimized_0.pdf.

Paul, S. 1998. The Performance of the Integrated Rural Development Program in India: An Assessment. *Developing Economies* 36 (2): 117–31.

Peters, J., M. Sievert, and C. Vance. 2013. "Firm Performance and Electricity Usage in Small Manufacturing and Service Firms in Ghana." In *Productive Use of*

Energy–PRODUSE: Measuring Impacts of Electrification on Small and Micro-Enterprises in Sub-Saharan Africa, edited by Lucius Mayer-Tasch, Mohua Mukherjee, and Kilian Reiche. Eschborn, Germany: Deutsche Gesellschaft für Internationale Zusammenarbeit (GIZ) GmbH. http://produse.org/imglib/downloads/PRODUSE_study/PRODUSE%20Study_Case%20Study%20Ghana.pdf.

Qadeer, M. A., M. Rashid, and I. Babar. 1977. "An Evaluation of the Integrated Rural Development Programme." Monographs in the Economics of Development No. 19, Pakistan Institute of Development Economics, Karachi. https://opendocs.ids.ac.uk/opendocs/bitstream/handle/123456789/2066/Monographs19-224155.pdf?sequence=1.

Ruttan, V. W. 1984. "Integrated Rural Development Programmes: A Historical Perspective." *World Development* 12 (4): 393–94. https://www.sciencedirect.com/science/article/pii/0305750X84900172/pdf?md5=1ceff13a8cb6e7c110ef90af386f3451&pid=1-s2.0-0305750X84900172-main.pdf&_valck=1.

Squires, T. 2015. "The Impact of Access to Electricity on Education: Evidence from Honduras." Unpublished.

Chapter 6

The Way Forward: Conclusions and Recommendations

Sub-Saharan Africa (hereafter Africa or SSA) faces significant challenges to expanding access to electricity and making it more reliable. The region is also confronted with four key trends that will have major ramifications for how it deals with the challenges.

- First, climate change poses a trade-off between what some analysts consider the cheaper option of the status quo of fossil fuels versus a more concerted move toward a renewable energy future. This trade-off also affects the type of electricity access and consumption, as well as productive use potential.
- Second, drops in the prices of solar technology, including mini-grids and systems that allow tier 4 and tier 5 access, will affect the spatial planning of grid electrification, especially rural electrification.[1]
- Third, ongoing rapid urbanization in African countries may have a significant impact on how one thinks about grid expansion. Conversely, electrification could also help slow the pace of urbanization through the buildup of secondary cities.
- Fourth, greater regional cooperation, such as regional power pools, can lower investment costs if the right political will is present. These trends will require forward thinking and careful planning among the various stakeholders.

Figure 6.1 depicts a conceptual framework for considering the roles of different stakeholders and the actions that would help accelerate progress toward access to electricity. The centerpiece of this effort starts with governments' need to have the right regulatory conditions in place to attract investment in all areas of the sector, including generation, transmission infrastructure, distribution, and operational management.

The private sector is needed to fill the investment gaps in the electricity sector, and for greater effectiveness, investment in complementary factors should

Figure 6.1 Role of Stakeholders and Actions to Accelerate Progress toward Access to Electricity

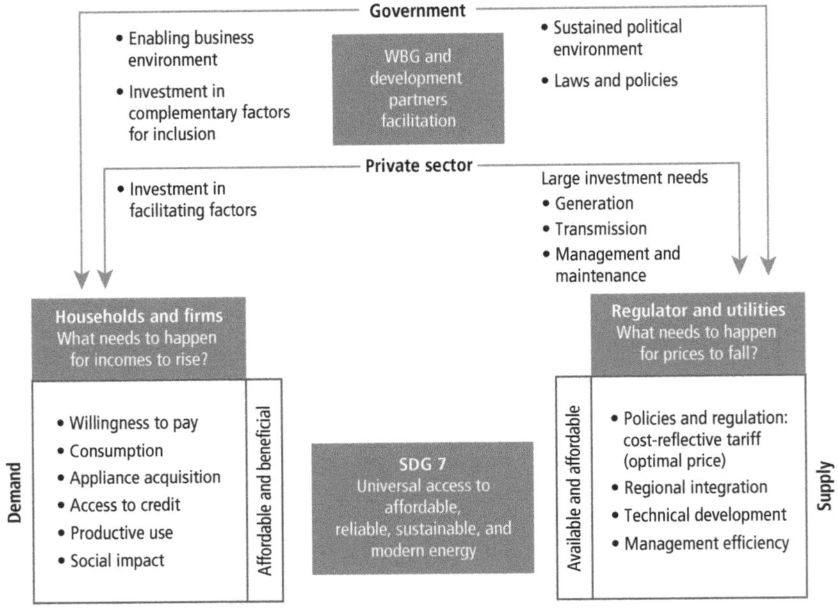

Note: WBG = World Bank Group; SDG = Sustainable Development Goal.

be pursued simultaneously (box 6.1). Governments should coordinate actions to attract private sector investment to those enabling factors that will help consumers use electricity for positive impact on the economy and their lives. That may include a deepening of the financial sector or infrastructure, such as roads linking large cities and connecting communities to markets and large urban centers. However, some of those complementary factors may not always be attractive for private investors or might be part of the prerogative of the government. Those areas may include supporting, mechanizing, and modernizing the often large and informal economies, or investing in skills.

Development partners can play a crucial role where needed to help facilitate the interaction between private investors and governments, from providing technical assistance for electrification planning to supporting building up the right regulatory environment, and from providing concessional financing to risk mitigation for drought, oil price shocks, and conflicts. This concerted effort should lead to falling prices for electricity coupled with rising household incomes, making access more affordable to a more significant share of the population at cost-reflective tariffs that allow utilities to be financially viable.

BOX 6.1

How Has Ghana Achieved High Uptake?

The experience of Ghana demonstrates the need for efforts on the demand side in addition to addressing the supply dimension. Ghana undertook a comprehensive National Electrification Planning Study between 1989 and 1991, taking into consideration all possible options for electrification, including grid and off-grid extensions as well as renewable energy–based solutions (biomass, solar, wind, and small hydro). This effort led to a master plan that outlined six five-year implementation phases over 30 years (1990–2020). The National Electrification Scheme aimed at connecting all communities with populations greater than 500 to the national grid as part of the overall goal of universal access to electricity by 2020. At the time, there were 4,221 communities in Ghana with populations of more than 500, of which only 478 had access to electricity.

Several demand-side initiatives were launched to spur uptake. Connection fees were lowered, and the government launched a complementary program called the Self-Help Electrification Program (SHEP) to speed up the process by electrifying towns and villages that were prepared to help themselves. SHEP is a rolling, three- to five-year electrification program, targeting communities that are not scheduled for immediate connection to the national grid but that are located within 20 kilometers of an existing medium-tension electricity line (11 or 33 kilovolt network suitable for further extension). Under this scheme, communities help the electricity operator lower its cost by erecting low-voltage distribution poles, thereby ensuring at least 30 percent of the households in the community are wired and ready to be served as soon as the electricity supply becomes available. Communities accomplish this work through a village electrification committee, which is responsible for mobilizing funds, establishing rights of way, and helping people wire their homes.

In 2000, an additional component for credit provision for income-generating uses of electricity was incorporated, to increase consumption and ensure the viability of the utilities. Recently, the same credit facility has been used to assist households in paying for their wiring. To assist with affordability for residential consumers, a lifeline tariff was set for people who use up to 50 kilowatt hours per month.

By 2005, the access rate reached 54 percent, and 3,026 towns and communities were electrified. Moreover, Ghana's rapid progress in poverty reduction seems to have been correlated with progress in access to electricity across the country, potentially alleviating affordability issues along the way. According to the World Bank's World Development Indicators data, Ghana experienced a sharp decline in the poverty rate, from close to 50 percent in the 1990s to 14 percent in 2012 (figure B6.1.1).

(continued next page)

BOX 6.1 (continued)

Figure B6.1.1 **Ghana: Access to Electricity and Evolution of the Poverty Rate**

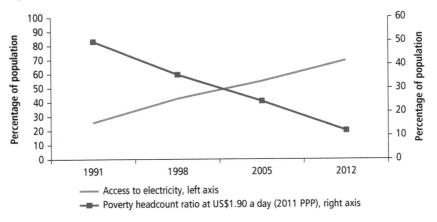

Source: World Development Indicators.
Note: PPP = purchasing power parity.

Key Overarching Policy Implications

Electrification needs to be economy centered and equity conscious. Focusing on enhancing the economic capabilities of communities is the best way to achieve faster progress while addressing the broad sectoral challenges (unaffordability, low consumption, the financial viability of the utilities, and so on). However, it needs to be equitable between urban and rural areas. The urban and rural access gap is too large to be rationalized because many rural areas have high economic potential—particularly in agriculture (for example, off-season farming and value-added agro-processing)—that must be explored, identified, and targeted following the same principle of enabling and enhancing the economic capabilities of communities. There are several overarching policy implications for boosting access, increasing uptake, improving reliability, and raising impacts.

- *Recognize that electrification is a long-term investment and a necessary input for long-term economic transformation.* Plans to increase access should not be evaluated based on short-term benefits only. African countries have underinvested in electricity even though in many countries, rents from natural resources could be an essential source of financing for electrification. The short-term benefits of electrification are unlikely to cover the development costs in the short run, but in the long run, electrification is a critical investment for sustainable economic progress. Delaying electrification has a high opportunity cost because the lack of electricity impedes modern technology adoption and lowers the quality of delivery of services such as health care, education, and many government services. It may also negatively affect how urbanization unfolds. Hence, finding ways to finance the upfront costs of electrification, which will pay for itself only in the long run, is necessary. In this regard, electrification may be viewed as a time-consistent way to save or invest for future generations.

- *Address demand constraints at all stages of the electrification process.* Addressing demand constraints is essential to raising uptake. Households in Africa typically cannot afford connection fees and high consumption tariffs because of lack of adequate and regular income. Households also face other demand constraints such as inadequate housing quality and costs associated with internal wiring—in addition to the inability to afford appliances. Many of these constraints may be and have been addressed by the deployment of technologies, such as smart meters, payment flexibility, and ready boards to circumvent housing quality requirements. However, it is important to recognize that these constraints are often symptoms rather than root causes of the deficit in electricity access. Addressing the causes will require focusing on enhancing economic impacts, which requires at least the following considerations:

  - *Target and promote productive use* so that electrification will raise household income, help with the financial viability of utilities through higher consumption, enhance household ability to pay, and feed back into public finance through taxes for reinvestment. These goals will, however, require reliability and the provision of complementary factors.

  - *Prioritize reliability,* whenever access is provided, because reliability will be crucial if electricity provision is going to pay for itself. Access rate alone should not be the sole measure of progress because universal access may not deliver its full promise if *quality* and *reliability* continue to be poor, with a significant strain on African economies and the livelihoods of their people.

  - *Coordinate with other sectors to take advantage of complementarities* and the provision of complementary inputs to productive economic activities. For example, coordinating with development initiatives (such as road infrastructure investment, access to finance, skills development, public service delivery) could provide insight into where to prioritize the provision of electricity, and thereby amplify its economic impact. Technology, such as geographic information system mapping techniques, can be leveraged to improve geospatial planning for electrification rollout.[2]

- *Take advantage of recent rapid technological advances to provide a variety of different forms of electricity service to meet basic needs and to strategically promote productive uses.* Stand-alone solar solutions provide services such as lighting, charging of cell phones, and power for low-capacity appliances.

Countries that seek to achieve such objectives faster and in a cost-effective manner need not wait for grid expansion. However, further technological progress will be required to cost effectively support productive uses such as off-season farming, value-added agro-processing, and promoting other small businesses (for instance, hairdressers, eating establishments, tailors).

• *Rethink government strategies for the sector based on the fundamental principles listed above and elevate understanding of key megatrends that may affect electrification rollout.* Experiences elsewhere indicate that the centerpiece of successful electrification rollout is the preparation and practical implementation in each country of a national electrification strategy that addresses in a systematic and coordinated manner the institutional, technical, and financial aspects of electrification. A recent study (World Bank 2017) finds that only half of 35 countries in Africa have an officially approved electrification plan. An adequate regulatory framework will also help attract investment to fill the gap where public funding falls short. However, 8 of the 10 poorest performers with regard to regulatory framework are African countries, underscoring the need for institutional reform and human and financial capacity assistance. Additionally, in the current era and in the context of African countries, megatrends that could affect the efficiency of electrification efforts should be factored in. These trends are *urbanization, technological change,* and *regional integration,* as well as *climate change.* There is significant uncertainty about the evolution and timing of these factors, which complicates electrification planning. All power sector planning and development should take into account the extent and impact of these trends.

Notes

1. Additionally, innovations such as smart meters, smart grids, distributed storage, and data analysis could lower costs, thus reducing investment requirements.
2. GIS-based support for the Energy Access Report: https://collaboration.worldbank .org/content/usergenerated/asi/cloud/attachments/sites/collaboration-for -development/en/groups/energyaccess/documents/jcr:content/content/primary /blog/_2012_euei_pdf_ghan-Q6Ck/-2012-EUEI-PDF-Ghana-GIS-based-support -for-Energy-Access-Report.pdf.

Reference

World Bank. 2017. *Regulatory Indicators for Sustainable Energy.* Washington, DC: World Bank.